I am pleased that JIF® is offering *The Peanut Butter Cookbook*. Now your families can enjoy the delicious and nutritious qualities of peanut butter with these easy-to-follow recipes. I highly recommend JIF because it tastes more like fresh peanuts. This superior peanut taste, which comes mainly from JIF's roasting process, will give more peanut flavor to your cooking.

*William J. Kaufman*

---

® JIF is a registered trademark of The Procter & Gamble Company.

# The Peanut Butter Cookbook

*William I. Kaufman*

SIMON AND SCHUSTER
NEW YORK

COPYRIGHT © 1977 BY WILLIAM I. KAUFMAN
ALL RIGHTS RESERVED
INCLUDING THE RIGHT OF REPRODUCTION
IN WHOLE OR IN PART IN ANY FORM
PUBLISHED BY SIMON AND SCHUSTER
A DIVISION OF GULF & WESTERN CORPORATION
SIMON & SCHUSTER BUILDING
ROCKEFELLER CENTER
1230 AVENUE OF THE AMERICAS
NEW YORK, NEW YORK 10020

MANUFACTURED IN THE UNITED STATES OF AMERICA

*I am grateful to the
Peanut Growers of Georgia and Alabama
for their assistance.*

# Contents

| | |
|---|---|
| FOREWORD | 9 |
| APPETIZERS AND SNACKS | 19 |
| SOUPS | 28 |
| MAIN DISHES | 32 |
| VEGETABLES | 63 |
| SALADS AND SALAD DRESSINGS | 75 |
| SAUCES | 82 |
| BREADS | 88 |
| COOKIES | 99 |
| CAKES | 124 |
| DESSERTS | 139 |
| CANDY | 151 |
| BEVERAGES | 162 |
| FAMOUS FAVORITES | 166 |
| INDEX | 177 |

# FOREWORD

If you can imagine two grown men sitting and having a business luncheon, discussing their preference for creamy or chunky peanut butter, you can understand how the idea for *The Peanut Butter Cookbook* was born.

When I indicated to my friend that I used peanut butter in a multitude of recipes ranging from sauces and salad dressings to baked goods and casseroles, he encouraged me to develop this book. *The Peanut Butter Cookbook* is for all who are looking for new cooking challenges and especially for those who want to put high protein into their diet at low cost.

Before telling you about peanut butter's beginnings in the United States, I should like to tell you a bit about the history of the peanut and its change from a simple legume used by few to one of the major agricultural crops in America.

Peanuts were among the previously unknown foods that the earliest Europeans who followed Columbus to the New World found growing in South America. One Garcilaso de la Vega reported that the Incas of Peru cultivated and roasted peanuts, which they called "Ynchic," long before the arrival of the Spanish. De la

Vega, son of a Spanish governor and an Incan princess, lived in the early 1500s. His history of the Incas and their predilection for peanuts was not published until 1609. He recorded that "Peanuts were good to eat if toasted, very good with treacle, and they make an excellent sweetmeat from it." The English translation of this work was published in 1869.

In his study of Inca history, published in 1653, a certain Father Bernabe Cobe stated, "Peanuts make good nougat, confection, and other gifts."

Jars that date back to 750 B.C. containing peanuts have been discovered in Peruvian-Inca tombs, and most authorities agree that sixteenth-century Spanish and Portuguese colonists introduced peanut or "groundnut" growing to Africa and Asia. It was from Africa that peanuts and peanut growing first made their way to the North American colonies in the seventeenth century, but peanuts were not much known beyond the borders of the South until after the Civil War when Yankee soldiers took home a liking for "goobers," a name by which peanuts are still known in peanut-growing country.

Although peanuts were cultivated in the South in colonial days, farmers did not produce them as a significant cash crop until 1915. A disaster to cotton farming, caused by the boll weevil, set the stage for this change in agricultural direction. George Washington Carver is credited to a large extent with convincing farmers to plant peanuts as one way to diversify their crops. Carver also emphasized the nutritional value of peanuts and dramatized their virtues by developing three hundred experimental uses for them.

More than half the United States peanut crop is grown in Georgia and Alabama where agricultural conditions are the most hospitable. Peanut farming requires four to five months of high temperatures, adequate rainfall and light-textured soil. Development of new varieties of peanuts can take as long as twelve years and the most successful new variety in modern times is the "Florunner." Introduced to commercial farming in the early 1970s, the Florunner's flavor and other qualities quickly made it the number one peanut used in peanut butter. It is the dominant peanut grown in both Georgia and Alabama, the states that supply about two-thirds of all the peanuts used in the peanut butter industry.

The peanut is a legume like peas and beans. The plant itself resembles a pea vine with light green leaves growing in a bunch plant about eighteen inches high or sprawled closer to the ground, if it is a runner type. After the blossoms fade, some of the stems of the blossom bury themselves in the ground where yellowish pods develop into shells containing one, two or three seeds. In harvesting, the plants are pulled from the ground and the peanuts in the shell are shaken off. Except for being cleaned and roasted, they look much the same as the roasted peanuts you buy in the supermarket or at the ballgame.

Although peanuts have been ground and mixed with honey or cocoa for centuries, peanut butter as a North American food did not appear on the scene until 1890. A doctor in St. Louis, seeking a nutritious, easily digested and high-protein food for some of his patients, "discovered" peanut butter. Soon homemakers were able to buy devices for roasting and grinding peanuts with which to make peanut butter in their own kitchens. By the early 1920s, peanut butter was known and appreciated by adults and children across the nation. This early peanut butter was much the same as that of the doctor in St. Louis—merely ground-up peanuts flavored with a little salt. The natural oil of the peanut would rise to the top of the container if it stood unused. Some vigorous stirring was required to remix the oil into the

## NUTRITIVE VALUE OF FAVORITE PROTEIN FOODS
(100 Grams, Edible Portion)

| FOOD ITEM (100 grams) | Protein grams | Food Energy calories | Fat grams | Calcium milligrams | Phosphorus milligrams | Iron milligrams | Niacin milligrams | Riboflavin milligrams | Thiamine milligrams |
|---|---|---|---|---|---|---|---|---|---|
| Peanut Butter (equiv. approx. 6 tablespoons) | 27.8 | 581 | 49.4 | 40 | 307 | 2.0 | 12.1 | .10 | .07 |
| Eggs, scrambled (approx. 1½ eggs) | 11.2 | 173 | 12.9 | 80 | 189 | 1.7 | .1 | .28 | .08 |
| Cottage Cheese, creamed (approx. ½ cup) | 13.6 | 106 | 4.2 | 94 | 152 | .3 | .1 | .25 | .03 |
| Tuna, canned, drained solids (⅝ cup) | 28.8 | 197 | 8.2 | (8) | 234 | 1.9 | 11.9 | .12 | .05 |
| Hamburger, cooked (3½ ounces) | 24.2 | 286 | 20.3 | 11 | 194 | 3.2 | 5.4 | .21 | .09 |
| Milk, whole, fluid (7 tablespoons) | 3.5 | 66 | 3.7 | 117 | 92 | trace | .1 | .17 | .03 |

ground peanuts. The mixture was stiffer than today's product and was not as easily spread.

Peanut butter has evolved from research begun in the 1920s at the same time it became a homemade comestible. One of the most important developments was the introduction of the use of stabilizers which prevent oil separation inside the jar. Another milestone was the establishment by the United States Food and Drug Administration of a "standard of identity" for peanut butter. This standard, effective in 1971, set up the following major requirements for any product sold as "peanut butter":

1. Peanuts must account for at least 90 percent of the content of peanut butter; the remaining ingredients to be limited to seasonings (salt, sweetener) and stabilizer.
2. No artificial flavors, colors, or chemical preservatives may be used.
3. Any product that falls short of the 90 percent peanut content, or fails to meet the other requirements, cannot be called peanut butter.

As a result of these government standards, some stores sell products labeled as "imitation peanut butter" or "peanut spread." They do not meet the USFDA requirements for real peanut butter.

Peanut butter is one of the nutritionally valuable foods available to the American public today. It contains about 26 percent protein, a percentage higher than eggs, dairy products, and many cuts of meat and fish, traditionally known as high-protein foods. Of the dozen or more high-ranking protein foods, peanut butter historically delivers more protein for the money than any of them except for dry beans.

In addition to its high protein content, peanut butter

is also a source of meaningful amounts of niacin plus such minerals as phosphorus and magnesium. Peanut butter is also cholesterol-free and has a high ratio of polyunsaturated to saturated fat.

There is no single food, not even peanut butter, that provides all the nutrients we need in our daily diet. That is why it is important to eat a variety of foods.

For example, the human body needs a daily supply of protein that provides necessary amino acids. Eight of the amino acids are called "essential" because they are the type that the body's own cells cannot manufacture and therefore must come from food. Protein foods from animal sources contain all eight essential amino acids. Vegetable protein foods, such as peanut butter, do not provide every one of the eight at optimum levels.

At any rate, peanut butter is a good source of protein, and the very few amino acids in which it lags do not pose a problem because of the nature of the American diet.

By combining peanut butter with some animal food such as a glass of milk, we get protein that is as good as that absorbed from all-animal food. For example: peanut butter as a sauce for meats; peanut butter combined with chicken; peanut butter used in salad dressing over shellfish. Using peanut butter in varying recipes provides us with an easy way to combine plant and animal protein in order to achieve favorable amounts of amino acids.

## HOW PEANUT BUTTER IS MADE

Peanuts are sold by the farmer to a sheller. The sheller, in his turn, shells, cleans and grades the kernels. Then he delivers them to the manufacturer. There are five separate steps in the peanut butter manufacturing process.

*Roasting.* Machinery must be specially designed for the roasting of peanuts for peanut butter. The process is a very meticulous one since it is in this stage that the flavor and color of the peanut butter are largely determined. Complete development of even color from the center of each kernel to the surface is sought. Scorching, excessive oiliness and decomposition of the surface fats must be prevented at all costs.

*Cooling.* When the peanuts are discharged from the roasting cylinder they are cooled quickly to prevent uneven development of color and excessive liberation of oil. This is achieved by powerful suction fans that pull large masses of air through the batch.

*Blanching.* By means of a rubbing action (as light or vigorous as necessary, depending upon type and quality of peanuts) the red outer skins are removed and blown into a collector. Skins can affect both the appearance and palatability of the peanut butter. The kernels are split, and the hearts are lifted out. The heart is a small, irregular piece of matter that contains the germ which, if it is not removed, tends to give a bitter taste to the finished peanut butter. The materials removed from the nuts during the blanching process are sold as by-products. Oil is procured from the skins while the hearts are utilized in the making of poultry feed and birdseed.

*Cleaning and Hand Picking.* Although the peanuts have already gone through a complicated hand-picking process and even been submitted to an electronically controlled sorting process at the sheller level, the two steps are repeated by the manufacturer to insure purity. A hand-picking table and a variety of pneumatic separating devices are used to remove all remaining foreign material and all shriveled or immature peanut kernels.

*Grinding.* In the final stage peanuts are passed through a set of grinding disks under uniform pressure to produce peanut butter. "Chunky" or crunchy peanut butter is produced by adding granulated peanuts to the finely ground peanut butter just before the jars are filled. Salt and other ingredients are added to most brands of peanut butter to prevent separation of the oil from the solid mass or to impart a distinctive flavor (honey or other sweeteners are common).

Irrespective of individual flavor differences, all manufacturers must abide by the federal regulations that demand a full 90 percent of peanut content in order for the product to be called good old lip-smacking peanut butter . . . one of our most valuable sources of protein as a snack, as a main dish sauce, a salad dressing ingredient, a dessert topping, or as the basic component of that delicacy known the world over, the legendary American peanut butter and jelly sandwich.

Peanut butter is the key to new cooking flavor and low-cost glowing good health.

—William I. Kaufman

# The Peanut Butter Cookbook

# Appetizers and Snacks

## MAHO BAY CAMP PÂTÉ

- 8 ounces raw chicken livers
- 2 tablespoons cooking liquid from chicken livers
- ¼ cup *Jif* creamy peanut butter
- 2 tablespoons Cognac
- ¾ teaspoon salt
- ¼ teaspoon nutmeg
- 1 teaspoon dry mustard
- 1 tablespoon grated onion
- ¼ cup finely chopped stuffed olives
- Dash Tabasco sauce

Wash the chicken livers. Place in a small saucepan and add just enough water to cover. Cover with lid and simmer for 15 minutes. Drain, reserving 2 tablespoons of the liquid. Put the livers through a sieve or finest blade of a grinder. Mix with the remaining ingredients, blending thoroughly. Pack mixture into a crock, cover and chill until needed. Serve with thin toast.

*Makes 1¾ cups*

## PAT GACK'S MEATBALLS

½ cup *Jif* creamy peanut butter
½ pound ground beef
¼ cup finely chopped onion or 2 teaspoons instant minced onion
2 tablespoons chili sauce
1 teaspoon salt
⅛ teaspoon pepper
1 egg, beaten
2 tablespoons peanut oil

Mix JIF peanut butter lightly with the beef, onion, chili sauce, salt, pepper and egg. Form into 36 small meatballs. Fry in the hot peanut oil, turning to brown on all sides. Serve hot with toothpicks.
*Makes 3 dozen*


## HOT PEANUT AND ONION CANAPÉS

36 saltines or whole wheat crackers
1½ cups *Jif* creamy peanut butter
6 small white onions, each cut into 6 thin slices
9 slices American cheese, each slice cut into 4 squares

Spread the saltines with JIF peanut butter. Top each cracker with an onion slice. Place a square of cheese on each onion slice. Broil until cheese melts. Serve hot.
*Makes 3 dozen*

## PEANUT AND HAM STUFFED MUSHROOMS

1 can (4½ ounces) deviled ham
¼ cup minced celery
⅓ cup *Jif* creamy peanut butter
1 cup (4 ounces) grated sharp cheddar cheese
24 large mushroom caps
Radish slices

In a bowl, mix the ham, celery, JIF peanut butter and cheese. Use the mixture to stuff the mushrooms. Serve cold garnished with radish slices. The mushrooms can also be broiled or baked in a hot oven (400° F.) for 10 to 12 minutes, or until lightly browned, and served hot.

*Makes 2 dozen*


## CRUNCHY PEANUT OLIVES

36 pitted black olives
¼ cup *Jif* creamy peanut butter
2 packages (8 ounces each) cream cheese
½ cup milk
2 cups finely chopped salted peanuts

With a pastry bag fitted with a star tip, fill cavities in olives with JIF peanut butter. In a bowl, mash the cream cheese until fluffy. Gradually beat in the milk. Drop a ball of cheese mixture the size of a large olive on top of the chopped peanuts. Press an olive into the center of the ball. Press nuts into cheese, shaping cheese until it covers olive completely. Chill until ready to serve.

*Makes 3 dozen*

## PEANUT BUTTER DIP

½ cup Jif creamy peanut butter
1 cup sour cream
⅛ teaspoon salt
1 teaspoon horseradish
2 tablespoons prepared mustard
Potato chips, crackers, or vegetable sticks

Combine all ingredients and mix well. Serve with potato chips, crackers or vegetable sticks.

*Makes 1½ cups*

## PEANUT PINEAPPLE DIP

1 cup sour cream
1 cup creamed cottage cheese
⅔ cup pineapple preserves
⅔ cup finely chopped peanuts
Crackers or toast fingers

Combine all ingredients and stir until well blended. Chill. Serve with crackers or toast fingers.

*Makes 3⅓ cups*

# PEANUT BUTTER HAM PUFFS

1 egg yolk
½ cup Jif creamy peanut butter
½ cup ground ham
1 teaspoon grated onion
¼ teaspoon salt
1 egg white, stiffly beaten
30 round crackers

Beat the egg yolk well and mix with the JIF peanut butter, ham, onion and salt. Fold mixture into the beaten egg white. Put small spoonfuls on crackers and place on a baking sheet. Bake in a moderate oven (350° F.) for 10 minutes. Serve hot.
*Makes 2½ dozen*

# PEANUT BUTTER BACON CANAPÉS

6 slices bacon
¾ cup Jif creamy peanut butter
¾ cup well-drained pickle relish
2 packages (10 biscuits each) refrigerated biscuits

Fry bacon until crisp. Drain on absorbent paper and crumble. Mix the bacon, JIF peanut butter and pickle relish. Beat until well blended. Open biscuit cans and press biscuits into 3-inch rounds. Spoon 1 tablespoon of peanut butter filling onto each round. Moisten edges of dough with water. Fold over to enclose filling and press edges together with the tines of a fork. Prick top. Bake in a preheated hot oven (400° F.) for 10 to 12 minutes or until lightly browned. Serve warm.
*Makes 20*

## PEANUT BUTTER CHEESE DIP

½ cup chopped onion
1 cup chopped green pepper
1 clove garlic, chopped
2 tablespoons peanut oil
2 tomatoes, peeled, chopped
¾ cup tomato juice
¼ teaspoon thyme
¼ teaspoon oregano
½ bay leaf
½ teaspoon salt
⅛ teaspoon pepper
½ pound American cheddar cheese, grated
¾ cup *Jif* creamy peanut butter
Potato chips

Cook the onion, green pepper and garlic in the peanut oil until tender, but not browned. Add the tomatoes and tomato juice with the seasonings. Cover and cook over low heat for 10 minutes. Stir once or twice. Put mixture in the top of a double boiler and add the cheese and JIF peanut butter. Cook and stir over boiling water until cheese is melted and mixture is blended. Serve in a chafing dish with potato chips.

*Makes 1 quart*

## PEANUT BUTTER CHICKEN DIP

2 tablespoons peanut oil
¼ cup minced onion
¼ cup minced canned mushrooms
4 tablespoons flour
2 cups milk
¾ cup *Jif* creamy peanut butter
1 cup chopped cooked chicken
1 teaspoon salt
¼ teaspoon pepper
Crackers or melba toast

Heat the peanut oil and cook the onion and mushrooms for about 5 minutes. Stir in the flour. Gradually add the milk. Cook and stir over low heat until mixture boils and is thickened. Blend in the JIF peanut butter. Add chicken and seasonings. Serve in a chafing dish with crackers or melba toast.

*Makes about 4 cups*

## DIABLO PEANUT DIP

| | |
|---|---|
| 1 can (4½ ounces) deviled ham | 1 cup (½ pint) sour cream |
| ½ cup *Jif* creamy peanut butter | 1 tablespoon minced onion |
| | Raw vegetables or crackers |

Combine all ingredients and stir until well blended. Chill. Serve with crackers or raw vegetables such as cucumber or carrot slices, cauliflowerets, etc.

*Makes about 2 cups*

## PEANUT STICKS

| | |
|---|---|
| 8 slices thin sliced bread | 1½ tablespoons peanut oil |
| ½ cup *Jif* creamy peanut butter | 1 cup cornflake crumbs |

Trim crusts from bread and cut each slice into 3 or 4 finger-length pieces (depending on size of bread slices). Dry in a slow oven (300° F.) for 20 to 30 minutes. Do not let bread brown. Meanwhile, blend JIF peanut butter and oil. When bread is dry, spread all sides with peanut butter mixture. Roll in cornflake crumbs.

*Makes 24*

## PEANUT CHOPS

12 large slices rye bread
⅔ cup *Jif* creamy peanut butter
1⅓ cups milk
2 cups cornflake crumbs
¼ cup butter or margarine
¼ cup peanut oil
Maple syrup

With scissors or a sharp knife, trim rye bread slices until you have a piece of bread shaped like a pork chop. Combine JIF peanut butter with milk until mixture is smooth and the consistency of thick cream. Dip slices of bread into peanut butter mixture, allowing excess to run off. Cover with crumbs. Press crumbs firmly to make them adhere. In a large skillet, heat the butter and oil. Fry "chops" slowly until richly browned and crusty. Serve warm splashed with heated maple syrup.
*Makes 6 servings*

## PEANUT CHEESE ROLLS

1 package crescent rolls
1 jar Old English cheese spread
½ cup chopped stuffed olives
½ cup chopped peanuts

Open crescent rolls out to make squares. Spread with cheese. Sprinkle with olives and peanuts. Roll up each jelly-roll fashion and cut into 1-inch rolls. Bake in muffin tins in a moderate oven (350° F.) or until done. Serve hot.
*Makes 1 dozen rolls*

## MAHO BAY CAMP MUSHROOMS

1 can (4½ ounces) deviled ham
1 teaspoon instant minced onion
⅓ cup *Jif* creamy peanut butter
¼ cup catsup
12 large mushroom caps
Drained capers
Finely chopped parsley

Combine deviled ham, onion, JIF peanut butter and catsup. Blend well. Use mixture to stuff mushroom caps. Serve sprinkled with drained capers and finely chopped parsley.
*Makes 12*

## HOT BACON, HAM AND PEANUT ROLL-UPS

1 can (4½ ounces) deviled ham
⅓ cup *Jif* creamy peanut butter
12 slices firm white bread, crusts trimmed
12 slices bacon

Combine the deviled ham and JIF peanut butter; blend well. Roll bread with a rolling pin to flatten. Spread peanut butter mixture on bread slices. Roll up each slice and wrap tightly in wax paper. Chill. When ready to serve, cut each roll into 2 pieces. Wrap a half slice of bacon around each roll and fasten with a toothpick. Broil, turning occasionally until bacon is crisp on all sides. Serve while warm.
*Makes 24*

# Soups

## CREAM OF PEANUT SOUP

¼ cup butter
1 cup thinly sliced celery
1 medium-sized onion, chopped fine
2 tablespoons flour
2 quarts chicken stock or broth
1 cup *Jif* creamy peanut butter
1 cup light cream
Salt and pepper

In a large saucepan, melt the butter over low heat and add the celery and onion. Cook until tender but not browned. Add the flour and stir until mixture is smooth. Gradually add chicken broth and bring to a boil. Blend in the JIF peanut butter and simmer about 15 minutes. Stir in cream just before serving. Season to taste with salt and pepper.

*Makes 8 servings*

## PEANUT SOUP CREOLE

½ cup chopped onion
2 teaspoons peanut oil
1 tablespoon flour
1½ teaspoons salt
½ teaspoon celery salt

½ cup *Jif* creamy peanut butter
2 cups milk
2 cups tomato juice

In a saucepan, sauté the onion in the peanut oil until tender but not browned. Add flour and seasonings. Blend in the JIF peanut butter. Add the milk gradually, stirring to blend. Cook and stir until mixture comes to a boil and is thickened. Add the tomato juice and bring just to a boil. Serve hot.

*Makes about 5 servings*

## COLD PEANUT BUTTER VEGETABLE POTAGE

1 can (10¾ ounces) condensed cream of mushroom soup
1 soup can water
¼ cup *Jif* creamy peanut butter

1 teaspoon celery salt
1 can (10¾ ounces) condensed vegetable soup, undiluted
2 tablespoons fresh chopped chives

In a bowl, combine the mushroom soup, water, JIF peanut butter and celery salt, blending with a beater. Stir in the vegetable soup and chill. Serve sprinkled with chives.

*Makes 4 servings*

## CREAMY PEANUT TOMATO SOUP

1 can (10¾ ounces)
condensed tomato soup

¼ cup *Jif* creamy or crunchy
peanut butter
1½ soup cans milk

In a saucepan, stir the soup into the JIF peanut butter, a little at a time, until well blended; add milk. Heat, stirring occasionally.
*Makes about 3 cups*


## QUICK PEANUT SOUP

¼ cup finely chopped onion
1 tablespoon butter
½ cup *Jif* creamy peanut
butter
1 can (10¾ ounces)
condensed cream
of chicken soup
1 can (10¾ ounces)
condensed cream
of celery soup
2 soup cans milk

In a saucepan, cook the onion in the butter until tender but not browned. Stir in the JIF peanut butter and cook for several minutes more. Blend in soups and milk and heat.
*Makes 6 servings*

## SUDANESE SHORBA

- 2 tablespoons peanut oil
- 1 onion, chopped
- 2 cloves garlic, chopped
- 1-inch piece cinnamon stick
- ⅓ cup Jif creamy peanut butter
- 2 cans (10½ ounces each) condensed beef broth, undiluted
- 2 cups water
- Dash cardamom
- 2 tablespoons lemon juice
- Salt
- Pepper
- Finely chopped parsley

In a large saucepan, heat the peanut oil and sauté the onion and garlic until golden. Add the cinnamon and JIF peanut butter and stir until the JIF peanut butter is melted. Stir in the beef broth, water, cardamom and lemon juice. Stir over low heat until soup bubbles. Season to taste with salt and pepper. Remove the cinnamon stick and serve in soup bowls, sprinkled with finely chopped parsley.

*Makes 6 servings*

# Main Dishes

## CHICKEN-PEANUT ONE-DISH MEAL

- ¼ cup butter or margarine
- 1 onion, chopped
- ¼ pound fresh mushrooms, sliced
- 1 small green pepper, chopped
- 1 can (10¾ ounces) condensed cream of celery soup
- 1 can (10¾ ounces) condensed cream of chicken soup
- 1 cup milk
- 4 cups diced cooked chicken
- 1 package (10 ounces) frozen mixed vegetables
- 1 cup sifted all-purpose flour
- 2 teaspoons baking powder
- 2 eggs, beaten
- 4 strips bacon, fried until crisp and crumbled
- ⅓ cup chopped salted peanuts
- 1 cup grated sharp cheddar cheese (about 4 ounces)

Sauté the onion, mushrooms and green pepper in the butter until tender. Stir in the two soups and ½ cup of milk. Put the chicken and frozen vegetables (broken up) into a well-greased 2½-quart casserole. Pour the sauce evenly over the chicken and vegetables. Mix flour and baking powder. Add the eggs and remaining milk and stir only until the flour is moistened. Stir in the crumbled bacon and peanuts. Drop the mixture by teaspoonfuls on top of the chicken mixture. Bake in a preheated moderate oven (350° F.) for 40 to 45 minutes or until biscuit topping is brown. Remove from oven and sprinkle with the grated cheese. Replace in the oven and continue baking until cheese is melted.

*Makes 6 to 8 servings*

# CHICKEN PUNJAB

- ⅓ cup cornstarch
- 2 teaspoons paprika
- ½ teaspoon salt
- ½ teaspoon onion salt
- 1 broiler-fryer chicken (2½ pounds) cut in serving pieces
- ¾ cup peanut oil
- 1 medium-sized onion, minced
- 1 cup sliced celery
- 1 green pepper, cut in rings
- 1½ cups uncooked converted rice
- ½ cup *Jif* crunchy peanut butter
- 2 tablespoons soy sauce
- 2 tablespoons brown sugar
- ¾ cup water
- ¼ cup seedless raisins
- 1 can (1 pound 4 ounces) pineapple chunks with syrup

Combine the cornstarch, paprika, salt, and onion salt in a clean paper bag. Add the chicken pieces, two or three at a time, and shake until well coated. Heat ½ cup of the peanut oil in a large Dutch oven or extra-large skillet with a cover. Add the chicken pieces and cook over moderate heat until well browned, turning as needed, for about 15 minutes. Remove chicken and set aside. Add the remaining oil and heat. Add the onion, celery, and green pepper and toss over moderate heat until softened. Add the rice and toss to blend and coat with mixture. In a bowl, combine JIF peanut butter, soy sauce, brown sugar and water. Stir until blended. Add with raisins, pineapple chunks and syrup to rice mixture. Stir to combine and bring to a boil. Reduce heat to simmer. Place the browned chicken on top. Cover and cook slowly for 40 minutes or until rice is fluffy. Every 10 minutes raise cover and lift rice from bottom to prevent sticking. Add a little more water if needed. Taste rice before serving and add more salt and soy sauce if desired. Heap rice on platter and arrange chicken around and upon it.

*Makes 5 generous servings*

# CHICKEN PIE WITH SWEET POTATO-PEANUT CRUST

8 new potatoes, peeled
4 carrots, sliced
8 small white onions, peeled
1 cup sliced celery
4 cups diced cooked chicken
2 tablespoons chopped parsley
1½ cups chicken broth or juice drained from cooked vegetables
1 cup (½ pint) light cream
3 tablespoons all-purpose flour
½ teaspoon crumbled poultry seasoning
Salt and pepper

CRUST
1 cup sifted all-purpose flour
1 teaspoon baking powder
½ teaspoon salt
⅓ cup *Jif* creamy peanut butter
1 cup mashed sweet potato
1 egg

Cook new potatoes, carrots, onions and celery until tender but still crisp. Drain and reserve broth, if desired, for sauce in pot pie. Put chicken and vegetables and parsley into a greased 2½-quart casserole. In a saucepan, mix the chicken broth or vegetable broth with the cream. Slowly stir the flour into the broth mixture. Add the poultry seasoning. Cook over low heat, stirring constantly until mixture bubbles and thickens. Add salt and pepper to taste. Pour sauce over casserole. To prepare the crust, mix the flour, baking powder and salt. Cut in the JIF peanut butter until the mixture resembles coarse cornmeal. Add the sweet potato and egg. Stir until a soft dough is formed. Knead a few times on a lightly floured board. Roll to a ¼-inch thickness large enough to fit the top of the casserole. Put the dough over the chicken, fold over edges and crimp to seal. Prick top with a fork. Bake in a preheated moderate oven (350° F.) for 35 to 40 minutes or until crust is brown and crisp.

*Makes 8 servings*

## INDIVIDUAL STUFFED CHICKEN HALVES

1 small onion, chopped
½ cup sliced celery
¼ cup butter
1 package (8 ounces) cornbread stuffing
½ cup water or chicken broth
½ cup salted peanuts
3 1½-pound chickens, split into halves
Salt and pepper
½ cup melted butter or margarine
Paprika

Sauté the onion and celery in butter until golden

and tender. Stir into stuffing mix along with the pan drippings. Stir in the water or chicken broth and the peanuts. Sprinkle chicken pieces with salt and pepper. Place chicken halves skin side down in a shallow baking pan. Divide the stuffing mixture equally among the chicken halves. Spoon the stuffing onto the chicken and wrap the wings around the drumsticks to hold the stuffing in place. Brush chicken heavily with the melted butter. Sprinkle with paprika. Bake in a preheated moderate oven (350° F.) for 1 hour.

*Makes 6 servings*

## CHICKEN WITH PEANUT SAUCE

- 1 4-pound chicken, disjointed
- Seasoned flour
- ½ cup shortening
- 2 tablespoons chopped onions
- Pinch of garlic
- 3 cups chicken stock or water
- 1 small piece cinnamon stick
- ½ cup sherry wine
- 1 teaspoon sugar
- ½ cup *Jif* creamy peanut butter
- 2 tablespoons cornstarch
- Rice
- ¼ cup peanuts

Dust the chicken with seasoned flour. Sauté chicken in shortening until brown. Add the chopped onions and garlic; sauté a few minutes. Remove all grease from skillet. Add the chicken stock or water, cinnamon stick, sherry and sugar. Simmer until chicken is cooked. Remove chicken, add JIF peanut butter, simmer a few more minutes. If more stock is necessary add about 1 cup, stirring constantly. When peanut butter has blended in, add a little cornstarch and stir until sauce thickens slightly. Serve chicken and sauce with rice and peanuts.

*Makes 4 to 6 servings*

## CHICKEN MOAMBA

2 tablespoons peanut or other cooking oil
1 cup chopped onion
2 2½-pound broiler-fryer chickens, cut into quarters
2 teaspoons salt
¼ teaspoon pepper
¼ cup *Jif* creamy peanut butter
1½ cups water
4 yams, peeled and sliced

Sauté onion in oil in a thick aluminum 10-inch skillet until soft, but not brown. Add the chicken pieces, cover and cook over low heat for 15 minutes. Add the salt and pepper, JIF peanut butter, water and yam slices. Cover and continue cooking (stirring occasionally) for 20 minutes longer or until chicken is tender.

*Makes 8 servings*

## CHICKEN CUTLETS WITH SPICY PEANUT BUTTER SAUCE

6 boneless and skinless chicken breast halves
Salt and pepper
2 eggs
3 tablespoons *Jif* creamy peanut butter
2 cups cornflake crumbs
½ cup peanut oil
¼ cup butter or margarine
1 large onion, chopped
2 cloves garlic, chopped
3 tablespoons flour
3 cups tomato-vegetable juice
⅓ cup *Jif* creamy peanut butter
1 teaspoon salt
½ teaspoon Tabasco

Sprinkle chicken on all sides with salt and pepper. In a bowl, beat the eggs and 3 tablespoons of JIF peanut butter until well blended. Dip the chicken breasts into the egg mixture and coat on all sides, then dip chicken breasts into crumbs and coat on all sides, pressing crumbs to make them adhere firmly. Heat the peanut oil in a large skillet. Cook chicken slowly until brown and crusty on both sides. Remove chicken breasts to a warm oven (250° F.). In a saucepan, heat the butter and sauté the onion and garlic until lightly browned. Stir in the flour. Gradually stir in the tomato-vegetable juice, ⅓ cup JIF peanut butter, salt and Tabasco. Stir over low heat until sauce bubbles and thickens. Spoon hot sauce over chicken breasts.

*Makes 6 servings*

## CHICKEN DJAKARTA

½ cup minced onions
2 cloves garlic, minced
½ teaspoon dried ground chili pepper
½ cup Jif creamy peanut butter
1 teaspoon salt
1 tablespoon peanut oil
2 tablespoons soy sauce
1 cup water
2 tablespoons lemon juice
2 2½-pound broiler-fryers cut into eighths

Combine the onions with the garlic, chili pepper, JIF peanut butter and salt. Sauté in the peanut oil for 4 minutes. Add the soy sauce, water and lemon juice. Cook over low heat for 5 minutes. Cool. Marinate chicken in sauce for 1 hour. Broil the chicken for about 30 minutes 4 to 6 inches from source of heat. Turn the chicken frequently (every 2 to 3 minutes) and brush

# Main Dishes

each time with the marinade. Heat remaining marinade and serve as a sauce for the cooked chicken.

*Makes 8 servings*

## CHICKEN IN HONEY PEANUT BUTTER SAUCE

½ cup *Jif* creamy peanut butter
¼ cup honey
¼ cup soy sauce
1 onion, grated
1 clove garlic, chopped fine
1 cup beef stock
¼ teaspoon freshly ground black pepper
2 broiler-fryer chickens (2½ to 3 pounds each) quartered

Combine the JIF peanut butter, honey, soy sauce, onion, garlic, stock and pepper, stirring to blend. Place quartered chickens in a flat pan and spread with half the sauce. Let stand for several hours in the refrigerator. Cook over coals or under the broiler, basting with remainder of sauce, until tender, about 30 to 40 minutes, turning and basting several times during cooking.

*Makes 8 servings*

## BATTLEFIELD FUFU

1 can (5 ounces) boned chicken
2 tablespoons *Jif* creamy peanut butter
2 tablespoons butter
1 tablespoon soy sauce
2 dashes Tabasco
¼ cup milk
Hot cooked rice, noodles, or toast

Remove chicken from can and dice. Heat the JIF

peanut butter and butter until the butter melts. Add the soy sauce, Tabasco and milk. Cook over low heat, stirring constantly, until the sauce thickens. Stir chicken into sauce. Spoon over hot cooked rice, noodles, crisp toast or melba toast.

*Makes 1 to 2 servings*

## AFRICAN CHICKEN WITH GROUNDNUT SAUCE

1 6-pound roasting chicken
Salt and pepper

**SAUCE**
½ cup butter or margarine
1 clove garlic, minced
1 small onion, chopped
½ cup Jif creamy peanut butter
2 tablespoons flour
1 can (6 ounces) tomato paste
2 cans (10¾ ounces each) condensed chicken broth
Parsley, navel orange sections and banana chunks

Wash the chicken and pat dry. Sprinkle inside and out with salt and pepper. Roast on a rack in a shallow roasting pan in a moderate oven (350° F.) for 1 hour and 15 minutes, or until leg bone is easily moved. Prepare sauce while chicken is roasting. Sauté the garlic and onion in butter. Stir in the JIF peanut butter until smooth. Stir in flour. Combine the tomato paste with the chicken broth and beat until smooth. Gradually stir mixture into peanut butter sauce. Cook over low heat, stirring constantly until sauce bubbles and thickens. Spoon the sauce over the chicken and garnish with parsley sprigs, orange sections and banana chunks.

*Makes 6 servings*

## SPICY CHICKEN LIVERS SOUTHEAST

| | |
|---|---|
| ⅓ cup butter or margarine | 2 tablespoons cider vinegar |
| 1 pound chicken livers | 2 teaspoons Worcestershire sauce |
| 1 onion, finely chopped | Salt and pepper |
| 3 tablespoons *Jif* creamy peanut butter | Crisp buttered toast |
| 1 can (8 ounces) tomato sauce with mushrooms | |

Sauté the chicken livers and onions in butter until the livers are golden brown. Mix together the JIF peanut butter and tomato sauce. Pour over the livers. Add the vinegar and Worcestershire sauce. Heat until bubbly. Season to taste with salt and pepper. Spoon over crisp buttered toast.

*Makes 6 servings*

## GROUNDNUT STEW

| | |
|---|---|
| 2 pounds lamb for stew | 3 chili peppers, washed and seeded* |
| 3 large onions, sliced | 1 cup *Jif* creamy peanut butter |
| 1½ teaspoons salt | 2 cups bouillon |
| 3 cups water | 3 to 4 cups hot cooked rice |
| 3 large tomatoes, quartered | 6 hard-cooked eggs |

Combine the lamb and onions in a large saucepan.

---

\* If fresh chili peppers are not available, used dried peppers or those pickled in vinegar.

Add the salt and water. Cook over low heat for about 1 hour or until meat begins to get tender. In another pan, combine the tomatoes and chili peppers with ½ cup additional water. Cover and cook 8 to 10 minutes or until tomatoes and peppers are tender. Strain. Mix together the JIF peanut butter, tomatoes, and bouillon. Add to meat. Continue cooking over low heat until meat is tender. When ready to serve, put a mound of rice on each plate. Place a hard-cooked egg in the middle of the rice. Spoon stew and gravy over top of egg.

*Makes 6 servings*

## INDONESIAN LAMB KEBOBS

2 tablespoons *Jif* creamy peanut butter
½ cup bottled Italian dressing
1½ pounds boneless lamb shoulder or leg, cut into 1-inch cubes
Paprika
Rice
Tomatoes
Onions

Add the JIF peanut butter to the bottled dressing in a small mixing bowl. Beat with a wire whisk or fork until smooth and creamy. Pour dressing over meat in a shallow dish; toss to coat meat with dressing. Cover and marinate in the refrigerator for at least 2 hours, longer if desired, tossing meat occasionally in sauce. String meat onto skewers. Sprinkle with paprika. Broil 3 inches from source of heat, turning occasionally, for 10 to 15 minutes or until meat is cooked but still juicy. Serve immediately with rice, broiled tomatoes and heated frozen or canned french fried onions.

*Makes 4 servings*

**VARIATION:**

## INDONESIAN CHICKEN

2 tablespoons *Jif* creamy peanut butter
½ cup bottled Italian dressing
1 broiler-fryer, cut into serving pieces
Paprika

Marinate the chicken in the peanut butter dressing as above. Remove chicken from dressing and sprinkle with paprika. Place chicken skin side down in a foil-lined, preheated broiler pan. Broil 6 to 8 inches from heat for 20 minutes. Turn and broil 20 minutes longer or until fork-tender and browned.

*Makes 4 servings*

## BEEF BIRMINGHAM

2 tablespoons peanut oil
1 clove garlic, sliced
1 pound beef chuck, cut into thin strips
3 medium-sized onions, sliced
1 cup sliced celery
2 tablespoons *Jif* creamy peanut butter
2 tablespoons soy sauce
½ teaspoon sugar
1 cup beef stock or bouillon cube and water
Dash of freshly ground pepper
Hot cooked rice or noodles

Heat the oil in a skillet; add the garlic, beef, onions and celery. Sauté quickly until lightly browned. Reduce heat and add remaining ingredients. Cover and simmer over low heat for 1 hour or until meat is tender. Add more liquid during cooking if needed. Serve over hot cooked rice or noodles.

*Makes 4 servings*

## GHANIAN STEW

2 pounds boneless beef chuck, cut into 1-inch cubes
Salt and pepper
2 large onions, chopped
2 large tomatoes, chopped
3 cups water
3 beef bouillon cubes
½ cup *Jif* creamy peanut butter
2 tablespoons flour, mixed with ¼ cup water
Cooked rice or baked yams

Sprinkle beef cubes on all sides with salt and pepper. Place cubes in a large saucepan. Add the onions, tomatoes, water and bouillon cubes. Cover tightly and simmer for 1 to 1½ hours, or until beef is tender. Stir in the JIF peanut butter until melted. Stir in flour mixture. Cook over low heat until sauce bubbles and thickens. Season to taste with salt and pepper. Serve with cooked rice or baked yams.

*Makes 6 servings*

## SOUTHERN RAGOUT

1 pound stew beef
1 clove garlic, chopped
1 tablespoon peanut oil
4 tablespoons *Jif* creamy peanut butter
1 can (8 ounces) tomato sauce
2 cups water
1 teaspoon salt
Dash pepper
½ teaspoon oregano
¼ teaspoon monosodium glutamate
1 cup sliced onions
1 cup sliced carrots
3 cups hot cooked rice

Cut beef into thin strips. Sauté with garlic in oil

until browned. Stir in the JIF peanut butter, tomato sauce, water, seasonings and monosodium glutamate. Cover, simmer over low heat for about 1 hour or until meat is almost tender. Add the onions and carrots and cook 30 minutes longer. Add additional water as meat cooks, if necessary. Serve on hot rice.

*Makes 4 servings*

## SPICY CHUCK ROAST

1 chuck steak (about 4 pounds)
Salt and pepper
Garlic powder
Flour
4 strips bacon, chopped
2 large onions, chopped
1 can (10½ ounces) condensed beef broth
1 can (1 pound) tomatoes, chopped
¼ cup Jif creamy peanut butter

Sprinkle steak with salt, pepper and garlic powder. Coat steak with flour. Fry bacon until crisp in a Dutch oven or covered skillet. Remove crisp pieces and reserve. Brown steak in bacon drippings on all sides. Add the onions and beef broth. Cover and simmer for 1 hour. Add the tomatoes mixed with the JIF peanut butter. Simmer uncovered for 30 minutes longer, or until steak is tender. Remove steak and reserve in a warm place. Simmer sauce until thick. Season to taste with salt and pepper. Spoon the sauce over the steak and sprinkle crisp bacon pieces over top.

*Makes 4 to 6 servings*

## PEANUT MEAT TURNOVERS

| | |
|---|---|
| 1 pound ground chuck | ½ teaspoon garlic powder |
| ⅓ cup *Jif* creamy peanut butter | 1 teaspoon salt |
| | ¼ teaspoon pepper |
| 1 tablespoon cold water | 1 package (11 ounces) pie crust mix |
| 1 teaspoon white horseradish | |
| | Peanut oil |
| 1 teaspoon soy sauce | |

Combine all ingredients except the pie crust mix and peanut oil. Mix well until blended. Shape the mixture into 25 small meatballs. Prepare the pie crust mix according to package directions. Roll out dough on a lightly floured board into a 15-inch square. Cut into 25 3-inch squares. Place one meatball on each square of dough. Brush edges with cold water. Fold over dough to shape into triangles or oblongs. Press edges firmly to seal. Chill for 1 hour. Fry in deep peanut oil preheated to 380° F. for 5 to 6 minutes or until richly browned. Drain on absorbent paper. Serve hot.
*Makes 25*

## PEANUT BUTTER PROTEIN BURGERS

| | |
|---|---|
| 1 cup *Jif* creamy peanut butter | 1 egg |
| | 1 clove garlic, chopped |
| 3 cups cooked brown rice | 1 onion, minced |
| 1 cup (4 ounces) grated sharp cheddar cheese | Salt and pepper |
| | Dry breadcrumbs |
| ½ pound bacon, diced and fried until crisp | ¼ cup butter or margarine |

Combine the JIF peanut butter, rice, cheese, crisp bacon, egg, garlic and onion. Add salt and pepper to taste. Add dry breadcrumbs as necessary until mixture is thick enough to shape into 6 patties. Coat the patties with breadcrumbs. Heat the butter in a skillet and brown patties on both sides. Serve on a toasted hamburger bun with catsup and onion rings. Can also be served plain with vegetables and a salad.

*Makes 6 servings*

## PEANUT BUTTER-BEEF MEAT LOAF

½ cup Jif creamy peanut butter
½ cup dry breadcrumbs
½ cup tomato sauce
1 teaspoon salt
⅛ teaspoon pepper
1 egg, slightly beaten
¼ cup finely chopped onion
¾ pound ground beef chuck

Combine the JIF peanut butter, crumbs, tomato sauce, seasonings, egg and onion. Mix until blended. Add the meat and mix lightly. Shape into a loaf on a greased flat pan. Bake in a moderate oven (350° F.) for 1 hour. Serve with gravy made from the drippings.

*Makes 1 loaf*

## GROUNDNUT CHOP

¾ cup *Jif* creamy peanut butter
2 tablespoons peanut oil
2 teaspoons salt
½ teaspoon paprika
¼ teaspoon nutmeg
¼ teaspoon pepper
2 cups water
3 cups cubed cooked chicken or lamb (about 1-inch cubes)
Rice ring
Selected accompaniments: flaked coconut, currants, chutney, chopped peanuts

Blend the JIF peanut butter and peanut oil in a skillet. Stir in the salt, paprika, nutmeg and pepper. Place over low heat. Blend in the water, stirring vigorously with a wire whisk or spoon. Add the chicken or lamb. Cover and simmer, stirring occasionally, until thoroughly heated, about 10 minutes. Serve in a ring of cooked rice with a variety of accompaniments.

*Makes 6 servings*

## ROAST VEAL WITH PEANUT BUTTER SAUCE

1 boneless veal roast, about 4 pounds
Salt and pepper
Crumbled marjoram
6 bacon strips
¼ cup butter or margarine
1 small onion, chopped
⅓ cup finely chopped celery
2 tablespoons flour
1 can (1 pound) stewed tomatoes
⅓ cup *Jif* creamy peanut butter

Rub the veal with salt, pepper and marjoram. Place

roast on a rack in a shallow pan. Cover the roast with bacon strips. Roast in a slow oven (325° F.) for 1½ to 2 hours or until tender and well cooked. In a large skillet, melt the butter and sauté the onion and celery until tender. Stir in flour. Gradually stir in the tomatoes, chopping them into small pieces with a spoon. Stir in JIF peanut butter. Cook over low heat, stirring constantly until the sauce bubbles and thickens. Slice the veal and spoon sauce over slices.

*Makes 6 servings*

# VEAL CHOPS WITH SPICY PEANUT BUTTER SAUCE

6 loin veal chops, about 1 inch thick
Salt
Garlic powder
⅓ cup butter or margarine
1 onion, chopped
1 can (10¾ ounces) condensed chicken broth
1 can (1 pound) tomatoes, chopped and undrained
½ cup chopped celery
⅓ cup Jif creamy peanut butter
2 tablespoons chopped parsley

Sprinkle the veal on both sides with salt and garlic powder. Sauté the chops in butter in a large skillet until brown on both sides. Add the onion, chicken broth, tomatoes and celery. Cover and simmer until chops are tender, about 45 minutes. Remove chops to platter. Add the JIF peanut butter and parsley to the pan drippings. Simmer until sauce is smooth and thickened. Season to taste with salt. Spoon hot sauce over veal chops. Serve garnished with parsley sprigs.

*Makes 6 servings*

# PERUVIAN VEAL IN PEANUT SAUCE

2 pounds boneless veal shoulder or breast, cut into 1-inch cubes
Seasoned flour
½ cup peanut oil
1 onion, chopped
1 clove garlic, chopped
3 cups stock or water
2 cups solid-pack tomatoes
½ cup *Jif* creamy peanut butter
6 carrots, pared and quartered
1 package (10 oz.) frozen peas or 1 can (1 pound) peas, drained
2 tablespoons chopped parsley

Dust the veal in flour seasoned with salt and pepper. Brown slowly in hot peanut oil in a large Dutch oven. Add the onion and garlic. Sauté for 2 to 3 minutes. Pour off all fat from the pan. Add the stock, tomatoes and JIF peanut butter. Simmer, covered, for 1 hour, or until meat is almost tender. Add remaining ingredients. Simmer, covered, 15 to 20 minutes longer, or until carrots are tender. For thicker gravy, blend 1½ tablespoons of cornstarch to a smooth paste in 2 tablespoons of water. Stir into the hot liquid and cook, stirring occasionally, until gravy thickens and boils 1 minute.

*Makes 6 servings*

# PEANUT BUTTER STUFFED PORK CHOPS

6 pork chops, 1 inch thick
Salt
Poultry seasoning
1 cup fresh breadcrumbs
½ teaspoon salt
¼ teaspoon pepper
1 small onion, chopped
1 small apple, peeled, cored, and chopped
3 tablespoons *Jif* creamy peanut butter
¼ cup peanut oil
¼ cup catsup
1 can (10¾ ounces) condensed cream of potato soup
Rice, noodles, potatoes or pasta

Cut a pocket in the side of each pork chop. Sprinkle inside and out with salt and poultry seasoning. Combine the breadcrumbs, salt, pepper, onion, apple and JIF peanut butter. Use mixture to stuff chops. Skewer edges together with toothpicks. (This can be done ahead of time and the chops refrigerated until ready to be cooked.) Brown chops on both sides in hot peanut oil. Add the catsup and soup. Stir to blend. Cover. Simmer for about 1 hour or until chops are tender. Serve over rice, noodles, mashed potatoes, or the pasta of your preference.

*Makes 6 servings*

# GONE WITH THE WIND FRITTERS

- 2 cups sifted all-purpose flour
- 2½ teaspoons baking powder
- ½ teaspoon salt
- 3 eggs
- ½ cup milk
- 3 tablespoons peanut oil
- 1½ cups finely chopped smoked ham
- 1 cup drained kernel corn
- 1 tablespoon minced onion
- ½ cup chopped salted peanuts
- Deep peanut oil
- Tomato sauce

Mix the flour, baking powder and salt. Beat the eggs with milk and peanut oil. Add liquid all at once to the dry ingredients. Stir only until flour is moistened; the batter will be lumpy. Fold in the ham, corn, onion, and peanuts. Drop mixture by teaspoonfuls into preheated deep oil (380° F.) and fry for 3 to 4 minutes, turning to brown both sides. Drain on absorbent paper. Serve hot with your favorite tomato sauce.

*Makes 6 to 8 servings*

# BAKED HAM ROLLS GEORGIA

- 2 cups mashed sweet potatoes
- 3 tablespoons margarine, melted
- 8 large thin slices cooked ham
- 1 cup dark corn syrup
- ½ cup *Jif* creamy peanut butter
- ¼ cup orange juice
- 1 teaspoon grated orange rind

Combine the mashed sweet potatoes with 2 tablespoons of the melted margarine. Place about ¼ cup of the mixture on each ham slice. Roll up and fasten with wooden picks. Place in a shallow baking dish. Combine the remaining ingredients with remaining margarine. Pour over ham rolls. Bake in a moderate oven (350° F.) until heated, about 30 minutes, basting and turning occasionally.

*Makes 4 servings*

## PORK ROAST WITH BRAZILIAN PEANUT SAUCE

| | |
|---|---|
| 3 pounds loin or rib roast of pork | 1 quart stock or water |
| 1 onion, chopped | ¾ cup *Jif* creamy peanut butter |
| 4 tomatoes, peeled and chopped | 1 teaspoon salt |
| | ⅛ teaspoon pepper |

Roast the pork in a slow oven (325° F.) for about 1¼ hours or until well browned. Remove pork from pan; add the onion to pan and sauté a few minutes on top of range. Pour off all fat. Add the remaining ingredients to pan and bring to a boil, stirring constantly. Return the pork roast and simmer, covered, for 20 to 30 minutes or until pork is done. Place meat on a serving platter and keep hot. Beat sauce until smooth and serve over hot pork.

*Makes 4 servings*

# PORK CHOPS WITH SPICED FRUIT PEANUT STUFFING

12 pork chops, cut ½ inch thick
Salt and pepper
½ cup melted butter or margarine
1 onion, chopped
1 quart ½-inch cubes white bread
½ cup chopped celery
1 apple, cored, peeled and chopped
¾ cup orange juice
¼ cup Jif creamy peanut butter
½ teaspoon allspice
1 can (10¾ ounces) condensed cream of mushroom soup
⅓ cup water

Sprinkle pork chops with salt and pepper. Score fatty edges to prevent curling during cooking. Heat the butter and sauté the onion until golden. Add the bread cubes and sauté until bread cubes are brown. Toss with the celery and apple. Beat the orange juice, JIF peanut butter and allspice until blended. Pour mixture over bread and toss to coat all pieces. Put 6 pork chops into a shallow greased casserole large enough to fit chops side by side. Spoon some stuffing onto each chop. Top with the second layer of chops. Mix the soup and water; spoon sauce over chops. Cover and bake in a preheated moderate oven (350° F.) for 50 minutes to 1 hour or until chops are tender. Serve stuffed chops with some of the pan drippings spooned over them.

*Makes 6 servings*

# PEANUT BUTTER HUSH PUPPIES WITH FRIED TROUT

3 cups yellow cornmeal
2 teaspoons baking powder
1½ teaspoons salt
2 tablespoons minced instant onion
1 egg
1 cup milk
¼ cup *Jif* creamy peanut butter
1 cup tomato juice

Shallow peanut oil for frying
6 trout
Salt, pepper and lemon juice
1 egg, well beaten
2 cups cornflake crumbs
Fresh parsley
Lemon slices

Combine the cornmeal, baking powder, salt and onion. Beat the egg with the milk, JIF peanut butter and tomato juice; mix with the dry ingredients and set aside. Heat the oil. Clean and trim the trout; sprinkle inside and out with salt, pepper and lemon juice. Dip the trout into the beaten egg and then into the cornflake crumbs. Fry trout in the hot oil until golden brown on both sides. Add more oil when the trout is fried. Drop hush puppy batter by teaspoonfuls into the shallow oil. Fry for 2 to 3 minutes or until golden brown. Turn and brown on the other side. Drain on absorbent paper. Serve hot with the hot fried trout. Garnish with parsley and lemon slices.

*Makes 6 servings*

## SHRIMP TAHITI

2 tablespoons peanut oil
1¼ cups diced onion
2 tomatoes, peeled and diced
2 teaspoons salt
¼ teaspoon crushed red pepper
½ bay leaf
1 can (8 ounces) tomato sauce
2 pounds raw shrimp, shelled and deveined
½ cup hot water
½ cup Jif crunchy peanut butter
3 cups hot cooked rice

Heat the peanut oil in a large skillet. Sauté onion over low heat until tender but not browned. Add the tomatoes, salt, red pepper, bay leaf and tomato sauce. Cover and simmer 15 minutes. Add the shrimp. Blend the hot water with JIF peanut butter and add to mixture. Cover and simmer 10 minutes longer. Serve over hot rice.

*Makes 6 servings*


## OKEFENOKEE FISH FILLETS

1 pound frozen fish fillets, defrosted (sole, haddock or cod)
¼ cup Jif creamy peanut butter
2 tablespoons lemon juice
1 tablespoon instant minced onion
1 tablespoon dried parsley
1 tablespoon dried thyme
¼ cup prepared dry breadcrumbs

Arrange the fillets in a greased flat baking dish. Mix together the JIF peanut butter, lemon juice, onion, parsley and thyme. Spread on the fish fillets. Sprinkle with breadcrumbs. Bake in a moderate oven (375° F.) for 25 minutes.

*Makes 4 servings*

## PEANUT COUNTRY FISH FRY

2 pounds seafood (flounder pieces, smelts, scallops, shelled and deveined shrimp)
2 eggs
½ cup milk, beer or wine
1 cup all-purpose flour
1 teaspoon baking powder
1 teaspoon salt
1 tablespoon peanut oil
Peanut oil for frying

Dry seafood well. Beat the eggs, milk, flour, baking powder, salt and oil together until smooth. Dip the seafood pieces in the batter and then fry as directed below.

*To shallow fry:* fill a skillet with peanut oil 1½ inches deep. Heat oil until a cube of bread browns in 30 seconds. Drop seafood into oil. Fry 3 to 4 minutes on one side; turn and brown 3 to 4 minutes on the other side. Drain seafood on absorbent paper. Serve at once.

*To deep fry:* fill a deep saucepan or fryer with peanut oil to within 2 inches of the top. Heat oil to 380° F. using a fat frying thermometer to test the temperature. Drop the seafood into the oil and fry 5 to 6 minutes or until golden brown. Use a slotted spoon or large fork to remove seafood. Drain on absorbent paper. After frying is completed and peanut oil is cooled, it may be stored for reuse. Drain oil through a fine strainer into a wide-mouthed jar. Cover and store in the refrigerator. Label contents of the jar. When ready to reuse, add a little fresh peanut oil to the oil you have reserved.

*Makes 3 to 4 servings*

# CHICKEN AND SEAFOOD INDONESIA

| | |
|---|---|
| 1 4-pound chicken, quartered | 1 cup cooked crabmeat |
| 8 cups water | 1 cup cubed cooked ham |
| 2 leeks | 2 teaspoons ground coriander |
| 1 bay leaf | 1 teaspoon ground cumin |
| 2 sprigs parsley | ½ teaspoon ground red pepper |
| 2 teaspoons salt | ¼ teaspoon nutmeg |
| ½ cup peanut oil | 4 tablespoons *Jif* creamy peanut butter |
| 1¼ cups chopped onion | 1½ cups uncooked rice |
| 2 garlic cloves, minced | Salt and pepper |
| 2 cups chopped cooked shrimp | |

Put the chicken in a pot; add water and the leeks, bay leaf, parsley and salt. Cook for 1½ hours or until tender. Strain and reserve the stock. Remove meat from bone; cut into strips. (This may be done in advance.) Heat the peanut oil in a large casserole. Add the onions and garlic and sauté until tender but not browned. Add the chicken, shrimp, crabmeat, ham, seasonings and JIF peanut butter. Cook 10 minutes. Add 5 cups of the reserved chicken stock and the uncooked rice. Cover. Continue cooking for 12 to 15 minutes or until rice is tender and fluffy. Season to taste with salt and pepper.

*Makes 6 servings*

# PEANUT BUTTER LENTIL BURGERS

- 2 tablespoons butter or margarine
- 1 onion, chopped
- 3 cups cooked lentils or other beans
- ½ cup Jif creamy peanut butter
- ⅓ cup catsup
- 2 cups whole-wheat breadcrumbs
- Salt and pepper
- 1 egg, well beaten
- Wheat germ
- 3 tablespoons peanut oil

Sauté the onion in butter for 5 minutes. In a bowl, mash the lentils until pasty, then stir in the onions and drippings, JIF peanut butter, catsup, crumbs, and salt and pepper to taste. Shape mixture into 6 patties. Dip the patties into the beaten egg and then into the wheat germ. Heat the oil in a large skillet and fry the patties until brown on both sides. Serve on toasted hamburger buns with crisp bacon slices and pickle spears. Can also be served plain with vegetables and a salad.

*Makes 6 servings*

# PEANUT VEGETABLE LOAF

- 2 tablespoons peanut oil
- 1 large onion, chopped
- 1 cup chopped celery
- 1 cup finely chopped peanuts
- 1 package (8 ounces) cornbread stuffing mix
- 2 cups (8 ounces) sharp grated cheddar cheese
- 2 cups milk
- ⅓ cup Jif creamy peanut butter
- 4 eggs, beaten
- 1 teaspoon salt
- 2 cups cooked peas, drained

Sauté the onion and celery in oil until soft. Stir in the peanuts and stuffing mix. Add the cheese. Beat together the milk, JIF peanut butter, eggs and salt until smooth. Pour over bread mixture and let stand for 5 minutes until liquid is absorbed. Stir well, then gently mix in the peas. Pack into a heavily greased 9 × 5 × 3-inch loaf pan that has been lined with foil. Bake in a preheated moderate oven (350° F.) for 1 hour and 15 minutes. Unmold onto a platter and carefully strip off the foil. Cut into slices.

*Makes 8 servings*

## BAKED SPAGHETTI AUGUSTA

½ package (8 ounces) thin spaghetti
Boiling salted water
1½ cups milk
1 cup grated American cheese
2 tablespoons instant minced onion
¼ cup *Jif* creamy peanut butter
1 teaspoon salt
⅛ teaspoon pepper
1 teaspoon Worcestershire sauce
2 eggs, beaten
¼ cup chopped parsley

Cook the spaghetti in boiling salted water for 7 minutes. Drain. Heat milk to boiling. Add the remaining ingredients. Stir into the spaghetti. Turn into a greased 1-quart baking dish. Bake in a moderate oven (350° F.) for 20 minutes.

*Makes 4 servings*

# Vegetables

## PEANUT STUFFED PEPPERS

6 medium-sized green peppers
Boiling salted water
1 bar (10 ounces) sharp cheddar cheese, grated
2 eggs, well beaten
1 teaspoon salt
4 cups cooked brown rice
½ cup finely chopped celery
¼ cup finely chopped onion
⅓ cup *Jif* creamy peanut butter
1 can (16 ounces) tomato sauce

Slice the tops from the peppers and remove the seeds. Drop the peppers into boiling salted water and simmer for 5 minutes. Drain. In a bowl, combine the remaining ingredients except the tomato sauce. Mix until well blended. Use mixture to stuff the peppers. Place peppers side by side in a shallow baking pan. Pour the tomato sauce over the stuffed peppers. Bake in a preheated moderate oven (375° F.) for 35 to 40 minutes, or until peppers are tender.
*Makes 6 servings*

# LENTIL AND PEANUT STUFFED PEPPERS

1 pound lentils
1 tablespoon salt
2 tablespoons peanut oil
1 large onion, chopped
1 clove garlic, chopped
1 cup chopped celery
⅓ cup *Jif* creamy peanut butter
2 cans (10¾ ounces each) condensed tomato soup, undiluted
Salt and pepper
8 large green peppers
Boiling salted water

Cover lentils with water. Add 1 tablespoon of salt. Simmer for 45 minutes to 1 hour or until lentils are tender and easily squashed between fingers. Drain. In a skillet, heat the oil and sauté the onion, garlic and celery for 5 minutes. Stir in the JIF peanut butter and 1 can of tomato soup. Stir in the lentils. Season to taste with salt and pepper. Slice the tops from the peppers and remove the seeds. Drop the peppers into boiling salted water and simmer for 5 minutes. Drain. Stuff the peppers with the lentil mixture. Place the peppers side by side in a shallow baking pan. Spoon the remaining tomato soup over the peppers. Add ½ inch of water to the baking pan. Bake in a preheated moderate oven (350° F.) for 1 hour or until peppers are easily pierced.

*Makes 8 servings*

## AFRICAN SWEET POTATOES AND BANANAS

3 large sweet potatoes, cooked and peeled
½ cup *Jif* creamy peanut butter
Grated rind of 1 orange
3 firm bananas
⅓ cup firmly packed brown sugar
¼ cup butter or margarine

Cut the potatoes into halves lengthwise and place halves cut side up side by side in a greased shallow baking pan. Cut a thin slice from the bottom of the potato halves to allow them to stand straight. In a bowl, mix the JIF peanut butter and orange rind. Spread mixture over the tops of the potatoes. Peel the bananas and cut into halves lengthwise. Cut each half into halves crosswise. Place two halves on each potato. Sprinkle with brown sugar and dot with butter. Bake in a preheated moderate oven (350° F.) for 15 minutes or until brown and hot.

*Makes 6 servings*

## SOUTHERN SWEET POTATO-PEANUT BUTTER CASSEROLE

6 sweet potatoes, cooked, peeled and mashed
½ teaspoon ground mace
⅓ cup firmly packed brown sugar
½ cup butter or margarine, melted
½ cup *Jif* creamy peanut butter
3 navel oranges
¼ cup dry breadcrumbs
⅓ cup salted peanuts

Mix the mashed sweet potatoes, mace, brown sugar, half of the melted butter and the JIF peanut butter until smooth and well blended. With a sharp knife, slice and peel the white membrane from the oranges. Cut the oranges into ½-inch-thick crosswise slices. Layer the sweet potato mixture and orange slices in a greased 2-quart casserole, ending with the orange slices. Mix the breadcrumbs and peanuts with the remaining melted butter and spoon over the top. Bake in a preheated moderate oven (350° F.) for 25 to 30 minutes or until piping hot.

*Makes 8 servings*

## SIWEE

| | |
|---|---|
| 12 plantains or 6 sweet potatoes or yams | ½ cup *Jif* creamy peanut butter |
| 1 large onion, sliced | Salt to taste |
| ¼ cup peanut oil | |

Cook the plantains or potatoes in salted water to cover until tender. Peel and mash. In a saucepan, sauté the onion in oil. Stir in the mashed plantain and JIF peanut butter. Season to taste with salt. Stir over low heat until potatoes are piping hot.

*Makes 6 servings*

# STUFFED SWEET POTATOES WITH PEANUT BUTTER

4 medium-sized baked
   sweet potatoes
⅔ cup milk
¼ cup Jif creamy peanut
   butter
¼ teaspoon salt
Pepper
⅓ cup chopped salted
   peanuts

Cut the hot baked sweet potatoes in half and carefully remove the pulp from the shells. Mash thoroughly. Add the milk, JIF peanut butter and seasonings. Beat until fluffy and refill the shells. Sprinkle the chopped peanuts over the top. Bake on a baking sheet in a hot oven (425° F.) for 10–15 minutes or until brown.
*Makes 4 servings*

# PEANUT POTATOES AU GRATIN

¼ cup butter or margarine
3 egg yolks
4 cups hot mashed potatoes
Cream
Salt, pepper and ground
   nutmeg
½ cup finely chopped salted
   peanuts

**TOPPING**
3 egg whites
½ cup finely chopped sharp
   cheddar cheese
1 teaspoon prepared
   mustard

Beat the butter and egg yolks into the mashed potatoes. Beat in enough cream to make the potatoes fluffy. Season to taste with salt, pepper and nutmeg.

Fold in the peanuts. Spread the mixture into a well-greased 1½-quart casserole. Beat the egg whites until stiff. Fold in the cheese and mustard; spoon the topping over the casserole. Put casserole under broiler and broil 2 to 3 minutes or until topping is lightly browned.

*Makes 6 to 8 servings*

## PERUVIAN POTATOES SUPREME

- ½ cup Jif creamy peanut butter
- ⅔ cup heavy cream
- ⅓ cup milk
- ½ cup shredded Muenster cheese
- 2 tablespoons catsup
- ⅓ cup peanut oil
- ¼ to ½ teaspoon Tabasco
- Salt
- 6 medium-sized potatoes, cooked and peeled
- 6 iceberg lettuce leaves
- 6 hard-cooked eggs, shelled and sliced
- 12 large black olives

In a saucepan, combine the JIF peanut butter, heavy cream, milk, Muenster cheese, catsup and peanut oil. Stir over low heat until the sauce bubbles and becomes smooth. Add the Tabasco and the salt to taste. Place the boiled potatoes on the lettuce leaves. Add the sliced eggs and olives. Spoon the hot sauce over the potatoes. Serve at once.

*Makes 6 servings*

## SPINACH AFRIQUE

2 tablespoons peanut oil
2 large onions, chopped
3 ripe tomatoes, cored and diced
1 green pepper, chopped
2 packages (10 ounces each) frozen chopped spinach, thawed but not drained
½ cup *Jif* creamy peanut butter
1 chicken bouillon cube
¼ teaspoon Tabasco
Salt and pepper

In a large saucepan, sauté the onions in oil for 5 minutes or until golden brown. Add the tomatoes and green pepper. Stir over medium heat until the tomatoes are cooked and mushy. Stir in the spinach. Blend well. Stir in the JIF peanut butter, bouillon cube and Tabasco. Simmer, stirring constantly, for about 5 minutes or until the spinach is cooked. Season to taste with salt and pepper.
*Makes 6 servings*


## PEANUT FILLED ACORN SQUASH

3 acorn squash, halved and seeded
1 cup finely cubed bread
4 tablespoons butter or margarine
1 medium-sized tomato, peeled and diced
½ cup *Jif* creamy peanut butter
½ teaspoon salt
⅛ teaspoon pepper
⅛ teaspoon onion salt

Place squash cut side down on a greased flat baking pan. Bake in a moderate oven (350° F.) for 30 minutes. Meanwhile, sauté the bread cubes in 2 tablespoons of the butter until lightly browned. Toss with the remaining ingredients. Place partially baked squash cut side up. Brush with remaining butter. Fill with the bread mixture. Continue baking for 20 to 30 minutes.

*Makes 6 servings*

## PEANUTTY FESTIVAL SQUASH

2 pounds cooked mashed squash or 2 cans (1 pound each) pumpkin
1 jar (2 ounces) chopped pimento
2 tablespoons grated onion
2 grated carrots
1 can (10¾ ounces) condensed cream of chicken soup
1 cup sour cream
1 package (8 ounces) herb-seasoned stuffing
1 cup chopped peanuts
¼ pound margarine, melted

Combine the vegetables. Blend the undiluted soup with the sour cream; stir into the vegetable mixture. Toss the stuffing, chopped peanuts and margarine together. Turn half the stuffing into a shallow 3-quart baking dish. Pour the vegetable-sour cream mixture over the stuffing layer. Top with the remaining stuffing. Bake in a moderate oven (375° F.) for 30 minutes.

*Makes 8 to 10 servings*

# INDONESIAN VEGETABLE PLATTER

- 6 tablespoons *Jif* creamy peanut butter
- ¼ teaspoon garlic salt or 1 clove garlic crushed
- ½ teaspoon crushed red pepper
- 1 tablespoon lemon juice
- 1 teaspoon sugar
- 1 teaspoon salt
- 1 bay leaf
- 1 cup water
- ½ cup milk
- ½ cup shredded raw cabbage
- ½ cup sliced raw carrots
- ½ cup cooked green beans
- 2 tomatoes, sliced
- 1 cucumber, sliced
- Few lettuce leaves
- 2 hard-cooked eggs, sliced

Sauté the JIF peanut butter with the garlic and red pepper over low heat for about 3 minutes, stirring constantly. Add the lemon juice, sugar, salt, bay leaf, and blend in the water to make a smooth mixture. Add the milk and bring to a boil. Remove from heat but keep hot. Arrange the vegetables on a platter to form a pretty picture. Garnish with egg slices. Serve with a bowl of the hot dressing.

*Makes 4 servings*

# CAULIFLOWER WITH SPICY PEANUT BUTTER SAUCE

- 1 medium-sized head cauliflower, separated into flowerets
- ¼ cup margarine
- ½ cup *Jif* creamy peanut butter
- ¼ cup mayonnaise
- 1 tablespoon sugar
- 1 tablespoon lemon juice
- 1 teaspoon chili sauce
- ⅛ teaspoon hot pepper sauce

Parboil the cauliflower. Drain. Melt the margarine in a skillet. Add the cauliflower and sauté until lightly browned. Drain. Combine the JIF peanut butter, mayonnaise, sugar, lemon juice, chili sauce and hot pepper sauce in a bowl. Spoon on top of the hot cauliflower and serve immediately.

*Makes 4 servings*

## PEANUT-SAUCED CARROTS AND CELERY

2 tablespoons peanut oil
2 tablespoons flour
1 tablespoon *Jif* creamy peanut butter
¼ teaspoon salt
Dash of pepper
1 cup milk
½ cup chopped peanuts
1½ cups cooked sliced carrots, drained
1½ cups cooked sliced celery, drained

Blend the oil, flour, JIF peanut butter, salt and pepper. Gradually stir in the milk. Cook over low heat, stirring constantly, until thick and smooth. Mix with the peanuts and vegetables. Reheat until bubbly. Pour into a serving dish. Sprinkle with additional peanuts, if desired.

*Makes 4 servings*

## BRUSSELS SPROUTS WITH PEANUTS

1 quart fresh Brussels sprouts
2 tablespoons butter or margarine
½ cup chopped salted peanuts
½ teaspoon salt

Trim the sprouts and wash thoroughly. Soak in cold, salted water for 30 minutes. Drain. Put into a 1-quart thick aluminum saucepan. Just cover with water. Place over medium-high heat. When cover is hot to touch, reduce heat to low and cook for 10 minutes. Stir, re-cover and cook 2 minutes longer. Drain. Meanwhile sauté the peanuts in butter. Add with salt to cooked sprouts and toss lightly.

*Makes 4 servings*

# BRAISED CELERY WITH PEANUT-SOY SAUCE

3 cups sliced celery
1 medium-sized onion, sliced
¼ cup water
¼ cup *Jif* creamy peanut butter
2 tablespoons soy sauce

Combine the celery, onion and water in a 1-quart saucepan. Cover and cook for 5 to 8 minutes. Remove the celery and onion to a warmed vegetable dish and keep hot. Add the JIF peanut butter and soy sauce to the liquid in the pan. Cook and stir to blend and heat. Add 3 to 4 tablespoons of water to thin the sauce. Pour sauce over cooked celery and onion.

*Makes 4 to 6 servings*

## BAKED STUFFED TOMATOES

6 medium-sized ripe
  tomatoes
½ cup Jif creamy peanut
  butter
¾ cup soft breadcrumbs
1 teaspoon salt
⅛ teaspoon freshly ground
  pepper
½ teaspoon oregano
2 tablespoons finely
  chopped onions
¼ cup finely diced celery

Remove the stem ends from the tomatoes. Cut a thin slice from the tops. With a spoon, remove the tomato pulp and chop. Mix the pulp with the JIF peanut butter and the remaining ingredients. Fill the tomato shells. Place in a greased flat baking dish and bake in a hot oven (400° F.) for 25 to 30 minutes.

*Makes 6 servings*

# Salads and Salad Dressings

## PEANUT BUTTER-CREAM CHEESE TOMATO SALAD

1 package (8 ounces) cream cheese
⅓ cup Jif creamy peanut butter
1 cup (½ pint) sour cream
½ cup salted peanuts
½ cup finely chopped celery
2 tablespoons frozen chopped chives
Salt
Tabasco
6 large tomatoes
Lettuce leaves

Cream the cheese until fluffy. Stir in the JIF peanut butter and sour cream. Fold in the peanuts, celery and chives. Season to taste with salt and Tabasco. Pour into a freezer container and freeze until almost hard. Scoop out the tomatoes and season inside with salt. Fill the tomatoes with spoons of the peanut butter mixture. Place the tomatoes on a bed of lettuce leaves and serve at once.

*Makes 6 servings*

## LAYERED PEANUT AND ORANGE SALAD

½ cup chopped raw peanuts
1 tablespoon butter or margarine
1 package (3 ounces) orange-pineapple gelatin
1 can (11 ounces) mandarin oranges, drained
¼ cup sliced maraschino cherries
1 package (3 ounces) cream cheese
Milk
2 teaspoons grated orange rind
Lettuce leaves

In a small skillet, stir the peanuts and butter until golden. Cool and set aside. Dissolve the gelatin according to package directions; chill until syrupy. Fold in the oranges and cherries. Pour mixture into a lightly greased 8-inch square pan. Chill until firm. Mash the cream cheese and gradually beat in the milk until soft and fluffy. Stir in the buttered peanuts and the orange rind. Cut the gelatin into 8 2 × 4-inch oblongs. Put 4 oblongs on lettuce leaves. Spread the cream cheese mixture over the top of the 4 oblongs. Top with the 4 remaining oblongs. Chill until ready to serve.

*Makes 4 servings*

## DIXIE POTATO SALAD

- ¼ cup cider vinegar
- ¼ cup peanut oil
- 1 teaspoon salt
- ¼ teaspoon pepper
- 3 cups diced, hot, cooked potatoes
- 1 cup diced celery
- ¼ cup chopped green onions
- 1 cup diced ham
- ½ cup mayonnaise
- ½ cup *Jif* peanut butter (creamy or crunchy)

In a bowl, combine the vinegar, oil, salt and pepper. Add the hot diced potatoes and mix lightly. Chill. When ready to serve, add the celery, onions and ham. Combine the mayonnaise and JIF peanut butter. Add to the potato mixture and toss lightly.

*Makes about 6 cups*


## FRUIT SALAD WITH PEANUT BUTTER-PINEAPPLE DRESSING

- Bite-sized pieces salad greens
- 1 small cantaloupe, peeled and cut into thin wedges
- 2 cups seedless green grapes
- 1 pint strawberries, hulled and halved
- 8 slices pineapple, cut into quarters, or 2 cups diced fresh pineapple
- 2 cups sliced cling peaches or 6 peaches, peeled, pitted and cut into slices
- 1 can (6 ounces) frozen concentrated pineapple juice, thawed
- ¼ cup *Jif* creamy peanut butter
- ¾ cup peanut oil

Fill a salad bowl with the salad greens. Arrange the

fruits in a pretty pattern over the greens. Chill until ready to serve. Combine the remaining ingredients and beat until smooth and well blended. Spoon salad dressing over each serving of fruit salad.

*Makes 8 servings*

## SPINACH SALAD WITH PEANUT DRESSING

**DRESSING**
- ¾ cup peanut oil
- ¼ cup wine vinegar
- 1 teaspoon salt
- 1 teaspoon sugar
- ¼ teaspoon pepper
- 1 clove garlic, minced
- 1 teaspoon dry mustard

**SALAD**
- 6 cups stemmed young spinach leaves, washed and drained
- 1 red onion, sliced
- 3 hard-cooked eggs, sliced
- ¼ cup crumbled crisp bacon (about 6 slices)
- ½ cup shelled peanuts

In a jar with a tight-fitting lid, mix the oil, vinegar, salt, sugar, pepper, garlic and mustard. Let stand at room temperature for at least 1 hour for the flavors to mingle. When ready to serve, place the spinach, onion, eggs, bacon and peanuts in a large salad bowl. Shake dressing until well blended. Pour over salad and toss until all particles are well coated. Serve at once.

*Makes 6 servings*

## STRAWBERRY-PEANUT MAYONNAISE

- ½ cup Jif creamy peanut butter
- ¼ cup mayonnaise
- ½ cup strawberry jam
- 3 tablespoons lemon juice
- Dash salt

*Salads and Salad Dressings* 79

Combine all ingredients, mixing lightly to blend. Chill. Serve as dressing with fruit salads.

*Makes 1½ cups*

## PLANTATION GRAPEFRUIT PEANUT BUTTER DRESSING

¼ cup cider vinegar
½ teaspoon salt
⅛ teaspoon freshly ground pepper

¾ cup peanut oil
2 tablespoons *Jif* creamy peanut butter
2 tablespoons rum

Combine the vinegar with the remaining ingredients in a container. Cover and shake vigorously until the JIF peanut butter is blended with the liquids. Serve with mixed greens and grapefruit sections.

*Makes 1¼ cups*

## PEANUT SURPRISE FRUIT DRESSING

½ cup *Jif* creamy peanut butter
1 package (3 ounces) cream cheese

2 tablespoons honey or sugar
1 tablespoon lemon juice
Dash of salt
¾ cup pineapple juice

Combine the JIF peanut butter with the cream cheese and stir until well blended. Beat in honey, lemon juice and salt. Gradually stir in the pineapple juice, blending well. Chill. Serve as dressing with fruit salads.

*Makes 1½ cups*

## PEANUT BUTTER THOUSAND ISLE DRESSING

½ cup *Jif* creamy peanut butter
½ cup mayonnaise
¼ cup chili sauce
1 tablespoon minced fresh or dried parsley
¼ cup minced celery
1 tablespoon cider vinegar
1 teaspoon minced onion
½ teaspoon salt
1 hard-cooked egg, chopped

Combine the JIF peanut butter, mayonnaise and chili sauce, stirring to blend. Stir in the remaining ingredients. Store in a covered container in the refrigerator. Excellent with lettuce heart salad, as a spread for meat sandwiches, or as a sauce with cold meats.
*Makes 1¾ cups*

## FRUIT SALAD DRESSING À LA DOTHAN

½ cup *Jif* creamy peanut butter
½ cup orange juice
½ cup pineapple juice or pineapple-grapefruit juice
¼ cup lemon juice
½ teaspoon salt
2 tablespoons honey or sugar

Blend the JIF peanut butter with part of the juices until smooth. Gradually add the remaining juice and the salt and honey, stirring until blended. Store in a covered container in the refrigerator.
*Makes 1½ cups*

## PEANUT BUTTER FRUIT SALAD FLUFF

½ cup *Jif* creamy peanut butter
½ cup marshmallow fluff
½ cup pineapple juice
1 tablespoon lemon juice
Dash salt

Blend the JIF peanut butter with the marshmallow fluff. Gradually fold in the juices, stirring to blend. Stir in the salt. Store in a covered container in the refrigerator.
*Makes 1⅓ cups*


## PEANUT BUTTER VEGETABLE DRESSING

½ cup *Jif* creamy peanut butter
½ cup tomato sauce
3 tablespoons cider vinegar
1½ teaspoons onion salt
½ teaspoon salt
½ teaspoon prepared mustard
1 tablespoon A-1 Sauce
1 cup peanut oil
1 clove garlic, halved

Combine the JIF peanut butter with the tomato sauce, vinegar and seasonings. Gradually stir in the oil, beating to blend. Add the garlic. Store, covered, in the refrigerator for several hours before using. The garlic may be removed after several days' storage, if desired.
*Makes 2 cups*

# Sauces

## BARBECUE SAUCE SAVANNAH

¼ cup *Jif* creamy peanut butter
1 clove garlic, grated
1 medium-sized onion, grated
1 tablespoon cider vinegar
1 tablespoon sugar
1 tablespoon soy sauce
¼ teaspoon crushed red pepper
1 can (8 ounces) tomato sauce
1 cup water
1 chicken bouillon cube

Mix the JIF peanut butter with the garlic, onion, vinegar, sugar and seasonings. Gradually stir in the tomato sauce and water, stirring to blend. Add the bouillon cube. Bring to a boil and simmer over low heat for 5 minutes. Use as a marinade and basting sauce for pork or chicken.

*Makes 2½ cups*

# PEANUT BUTTER CHICKEN BARBECUE SAUCE

4 tablespoons peanut oil
¼ cup chopped onion
1 clove garlic, chopped
¼ cup Jif creamy peanut butter
1 can (8 ounces) tomato sauce
1 tablespoon sugar
1 tablespoon vinegar
1 teaspoon chili powder
1 cup water

In a pan, heat the peanut oil. Add the onion and garlic and cook until tender but not browned. Add the remaining ingredients and stir to blend. Simmer, covered, for 5 minutes. Use as a marinade and basting sauce for chicken or spareribs.

*Makes 2¼ cups*


# HOT PEANUT SAUCE

½ cup Jif creamy peanut butter
2 tablespoons soy sauce
2 cloves garlic, minced
4 drops Tabasco
2 teaspoons water plus ½ cup water

Over low heat, blend JIF peanut butter, soy sauce, garlic, Tabasco and 2 teaspoons of water until smooth. Slowly blend in the remaining ½ cup of water, about 1 tablespoon at a time, blending mixture smooth after each addition. Use as a marinade or sauce for chicken, pork or beef. Serve hot.

*Makes 1 cup*

## PEANUT BUTTER SAUCE FOR MAIN DISHES

¼ pound butter
½ cup flour
1 quart chicken stock

1 cup *Jif* creamy peanut butter
½ pint heavy cream
¼ cup dry sherry

In a saucepan, melt the butter. Add the flour and stir until a paste is formed. Bring the chicken stock to a boil, then add the flour paste. Continue stirring until desired thickness is reached. Blend in the JIF peanut butter, cream and sherry. Simmer for 15 minutes. This sauce is ideal over stuffed boneless breast of chicken.
*Makes 6 cups*

## ALL-PURPOSE PEANUT BUTTER SAUCE FOR GAME

3 tablespoons butter or margarine
3 tablespoons flour
1 cup sour cream
⅓ cup *Jif* creamy peanut butter
1 cup milk

2 tablespoons chopped onion
½ cup tomato sauce
1 tablespoon chopped parsley
1 tablespoon chopped chives
4 juniper berries, crushed

Melt the butter and stir in the flour. Gradually stir in the sour cream, JIF peanut butter and milk. Add the remaining ingredients. Cook over low heat, stirring constantly until the mixture bubbles and thickens. Simmer for 5 minutes. Serve hot over slices of roasted game.

*Makes about 3 cups*

## SPICED PEANUT SAUCE

½ cup salted peanuts
2 tablespoons peanut oil
¼ cup chopped scallions
1 small clove garlic, chopped
2 cups chicken stock
1 teaspoon lime juice
1 tablespoon soy sauce
Dash ground ginger
Few drops Tabasco

Place nuts in a blender and grind until fine. Heat the oil in a large skillet and sauté the scallions and garlic until golden. Add the chicken stock and the ground peanuts. Add the remaining ingredients. Simmer for about 10 minutes, stirring occasionally, until sauce is thick. Serve hot. The sauce can be made ahead and reheated. Add a few drops of water to thin it to the right consistency. Serve over roast chicken or pork, sliced turkey, cauliflower, boiled onions, or ham slices.

*Makes 2 cups*

## PEANUT SAUCE PERUVIAN

2 onions, chopped
2 medium-sized fresh tomatoes, chopped
2 tablespoons peanut oil
1 cup chicken stock
⅔ cup milk
Dash of ground chili pepper
¼ pound cheese (cheddar, American, Swiss)
⅓ cup *Jif* creamy peanut butter

In a 1-quart aluminum saucepan, cook the onions and tomatoes in the hot peanut oil for 8 to 10 minutes. Add the remaining ingredients. Simmer, stirring constantly, until sauce thickens slightly. Blend in an electric blender, or press sauce through a sieve. Cool and chill well. Serve over cold cooked chicken, shrimp, or with an antipasto tray.

*Makes 6 servings*

## PEANUT BUTTER CHANTILLY SAUCE

¼ cup *Jif* creamy peanut butter
½ pint sour cream
1 teaspoon horseradish
1 teaspoon salt
Dash pepper
1 tablespoon lemon juice

Put the JIF peanut butter in a small bowl. Gradually mix in the sour cream until blended. Fold in the remaining ingredients. Serve with cooked broccoli, green beans, asparagus, carrots, or other cooked vegetables.

*Makes 1¼ cups*

## COCONUT-PEANUT SAUCE FOR KEBOBS #1

2 tablespoons grated onion
2 tablespoons peanut oil
1 tablespoon dark brown sugar
2 teaspoons lime juice
¼ cup *Jif* creamy peanut butter
1 cup Coconut Water*
Dash salt

* *Coconut Water:* 1 cup of boiling water should be poured over 1 cup of canned coconut flakes. Allow to stand 20 minutes. Strain to make 1 cup of coconut water.

Sauté the onion in the peanut oil for 5 to 10 minutes. Add the brown sugar, lime juice and JIF peanut butter. Blend well. Gradually add the coconut water, stirring constantly. Add the salt. Cook until sauce is thick and smooth, about 10 minutes. Serve hot with kebobs.

*Makes 1½ cups*

## COCONUT-PEANUT SAUCE FOR KEBOBS #2

½ cup Coconut Water\*
½ cup Jif creamy peanut butter
2 tablespoons lemon juice
2 tablespoons soy sauce
½ teaspoon Worcestershire sauce
Dash Tabasco
Dash salt

Blend all ingredients. Heat in a saucepan and serve hot with kebobs.

*Makes 1 cup*

---

\* *Coconut Water:* ½ cup of boiling water should be poured over ½ cup of canned coconut flakes. Allow to stand 20 minutes. Strain to make ½ cup of coconut water.

# Breads

## PEANUT BUTTER BREAD

¾ cup water
⅓ cup yellow cornmeal
½ teaspoon salt
⅓ cup *Jif* creamy peanut butter
2 tablespoons light molasses
1 egg
1 package (13¾ ounces) hot roll mix
¼ cup lukewarm water

Combine the ¾ cup of water, cornmeal and salt. Cook until slightly thickened. Stir the JIF peanut butter, molasses and egg into the cornmeal mixture, blending well. Cool to lukewarm. Remove the yeast from the package of hot roll mix and dissolve in ¼ cup of lukewarm water. Stir yeast into the peanut butter mixture. Stir in the flour from the hot roll mix. Knead on a lightly floured board until smooth and elastic. Let rise, covered, in a warm place until double in bulk. Knead again and roll on a lightly floured board or pastry cloth into a 9 × 12-inch oblong. Roll as for a jelly roll, starting at the 9-inch side, and place, seam side down, into a greased 9 × 5 × 3-inch loaf pan. Let rise again until double in bulk. Bake in a preheated moderate oven

# Breads

(350° F.) for 40 to 45 minutes, or until richly browned. Remove from pan and cool thoroughly on a rack before cutting into slices.

*Makes 1 loaf*

**VARIATIONS:**

*Raisin Braid:* Stir 1 cup of raisins into the dough when the flour is added. Knead and let rise as above. Knead dough again and cut dough into 3 pieces. Roll each piece into a 12-inch-long rope. Braid ropes together and place on a greased cookie sheet. Pinch ends tightly to seal. Let rise in a warm place until double in bulk. Bake in a preheated moderate oven (350° F.) for 35 to 40 minutes or until richly browned. Remove from pan and cool thoroughly on a rack. Sprinkle with confectioners' sugar.

*Makes 1 loaf*

*Orange Knots:* Stir the grated rind of 2 oranges into the dough when the flour is added. Knead and let rise as above. Knead dough again and cut into 24 pieces. Roll each piece into a rope 8 inches long. Tie each rope into a knot. Place on a greased cookie sheet and let rise until double in bulk. Bake in a preheated moderate oven (350° F.) for 15 to 20 minutes. To glaze, mix 1½ cups of confectioners' sugar with enough orange juice to make the consistency of heavy cream. Spoon over warm rolls.

*Makes 24 knots*

## PEANUT BUTTER BACON ONION BREAD

½ pound bacon, chopped
1 large onion, chopped
1 package (13¾ ounces) hot roll mix
¾ cup lukewarm water
⅓ cup *Jif* creamy peanut butter
1 egg
2 tablespoons bacon drippings

In a large skillet, fry the bacon until crisp. Add the onion and sauté over low heat, stirring occasionally until onions are soft. Drain fat, reserving 2 tablespoons. Cool the bacon and onions to lukewarm. Remove the yeast from the package of hot roll mix and dissolve in lukewarm water in a large bowl. Stir in the JIF peanut butter and egg. Stir in the bacon, onions, bacon drippings and the flour from the hot roll mix. Beat until it is a thick, well-blended dough. Cover and let rise in a warm place until double in bulk, about 1 hour. Knead dough on a lightly floured board until it is a smooth ball. Shape dough into a long roll and place in a greased 9 × 5 × 3-inch loaf pan. Let rise again in a warm place until double in bulk, about 30 to 40 minutes. Bake in a preheated moderate oven (350° F.) for 35 to 40 minutes or until loaf tests done. Remove from pan and cool thoroughly on a rack before cutting into slices.

*Makes 1 loaf*

# PEANUT BUTTER BACON BREAD

- ½ pound bacon, cooked and crumbled
- 2 cups sifted all-purpose flour
- 1 cup sugar
- 3 teaspoons baking powder
- ½ teaspoon salt
- 1 cup *Jif* creamy peanut butter
- 1 teaspoon butter, melted
- 1 cup milk
- 1 egg, slightly beaten
- 1 cup chopped peanuts

In a large skillet, fry the bacon until crisp; drain; crumble into small pieces. Stir together the flour, sugar, baking powder and salt. Cut in the JIF peanut butter until the mixture resembles coarse cornmeal. Combine the butter, milk and egg. Pour into the peanut butter mixture and mix thoroughly. Stir in the crumbled bacon and chopped peanuts. Pour into a greased and floured 9 × 5 × 3-inch loaf pan. Let stand 20 minutes. Bake in a slow oven (325° F.) for 1 hour and 15 minutes, or until loaf tests done. Cool on rack.

*Makes 1 loaf*

## PEANUT BUTTER PINWHEEL LOAF

2 envelopes active dry yeast
½ cup lukewarm water
½ cup butter or margarine
¼ cup sugar
2½ teaspoons salt
1 cup hot milk
2 eggs
Grated rind of 1 orange
5 to 5½ cups sifted all-purpose flour
½ cup *Jif* creamy peanut butter
½ cup orange marmalade
1 cup raisins
2 cups confectioners' sugar
¼ cup orange juice (about)

Dissolve the yeast in the lukewarm water. In a large bowl, combine the butter, sugar, salt and hot milk. Stir until the butter melts and the mixture cools to lukewarm. Stir in the yeast, eggs and orange rind. Stir in the flour until the dough is stiff. Knead dough on a lightly floured board for 5 minutes or until smooth and elastic. Replace in bowl, cover and let rise until double in bulk. Punch down dough and cut into 2 pieces. Roll out each piece on a lightly floured board to a 9 × 12-inch oblong. Spread each piece with half of the JIF peanut butter and then with half of the orange marmalade. Sprinkle with raisins. Roll up each piece, starting at the 9-inch side, like a jelly roll. Press ends of each roll together to seal. Place seam side down in 2 greased 9 × 5 × 3-inch loaf pans. Let rise again until double in bulk. Bake in a preheated moderate oven (350° F.) for 40 to 50 minutes or until loaves sound hollow when thumped. Remove from pans and cool on a rack. To glaze, mix the 2 cups of confectioners' sugar with about ¼ cup of orange juice to make the consistency of heavy cream. Spoon over warm loaves. Slice into "pinwheels."

*Makes two 9 × 5 × 3-inch loaves*

## GLAZED PEANUT BUTTER RAISIN LOAF

| | |
|---|---|
| 1 package (13¾ ounces) hot roll mix | ½ cup *Jif* crunchy peanut butter |
| ¾ cup lukewarm water | ½ cup raisins |
| 1 egg | 1 cup confectioners' sugar |
| 1 teaspoon ground cinnamon | 1 to 2 tablespoons milk |

Remove the yeast from the package of hot roll mix and dissolve in the lukewarm water. Beat in the egg and cinnamon. Stir in the flour to mix. Knead a few times to make dough into a smooth ball. Let rise, covered, in a warm place until double in bulk. On a lightly floured board, knead dough again and roll out to a 10-inch square. Spread dough with Jif peanut butter and sprinkle with raisins. Roll up like a jelly roll. Turn ends under to seal. Place seam side down in a greased 9 × 5 × 3-inch loaf pan. Let rise in a warm place until double in bulk. Bake in a preheated moderate oven (375° F.) for 40 to 45 minutes or until loaf sounds hollow when thumped. Unmold. To glaze, mix the 1 cup of confectioners' sugar with 1 to 2 tablespoons of milk. Spoon over warm loaf. Cool thoroughly before slicing.

*Makes one 9 × 5 × 3-inch loaf*

## BAMA PEANUT-BANANA BREAD WITH ORANGE GLAZE

¼ cup butter or margarine
⅓ cup *Jif* creamy peanut butter
2 eggs
¾ cup dark brown sugar, firmly packed
1 cup mashed ripe bananas (about 2 medium-sized)
Grated rind of 1 orange
½ cup milk
1½ cups unsifted all-purpose flour
½ teaspoon salt
1 teaspoon baking soda
1 cup peanuts, finely chopped
1½ cups confectioners' sugar
¼ cup orange juice (about)

In a bowl, cream the butter until fluffy. Stir in the JIF peanut butter, eggs and brown sugar. Beat until well blended. Stir in the bananas, orange rind and milk. Stir in the flour, salt and baking soda. Stir until well blended. Fold in the peanuts. Pour mixture into a well-greased 9 × 5 × 3-inch loaf pan. Bake in a preheated moderate oven (350° F.) for 1 hour or until loaf is richly browned. Remove from pan and cool on a rack. In a bowl, mix the confectioners' sugar with enough orange juice to make the consistency of heavy cream. Spread mixture over top of loaf, allowing excess to drip down sides.

*Makes one 9 × 5 × 3-inch loaf*

# TANGY FRUITBREAD

1 cup dates, chopped
½ cup dried apricots, chopped
½ cup raisins
Boiling water
1 egg
⅓ cup dark brown sugar, firmly packed
⅓ cup Jif creamy peanut butter
1 teaspoon vanilla
1⅓ cups sifted all-purpose flour
1 teaspoon baking soda
1 tablespoon grated orange rind
1 teaspoon ground nutmeg

Soak the dates, apricots and raisins in boiling water to cover. Set aside. In another large bowl, beat the egg until foamy. Stir in the brown sugar, JIF peanut butter and vanilla. Reserve ½ cup of the water in which the fruits have been soaking. Drain fruits well in a colander for a few minutes. Sift the flour and baking soda. Add the dry ingredients alternately with the reserved hot water, beginning and ending with the dry ingredients. Fold in the grated orange rind, nutmeg and drained fruits. Spread the batter evenly in a well-greased 8 × 8 × 2-inch pan. Bake in a preheated moderate oven (350° F.) for 35 to 40 minutes. Cool in pan on a rack. May be cut into squares and served for dessert topped with ice cream or frosting. After thorough cooling, it may be cut into ½-inch slices and served topped with cream cheese, butter, jam, or jellies.

*Makes one 8 × 8 × 2-inch square*

## PEANUT BUTTER WHEAT ROLLS

2 envelopes active dry yeast
2 cups lukewarm water
⅓ cup butter or margarine
1 cup *Jif* creamy peanut butter
4 cups all-purpose flour
1½ cups whole wheat flour
1 tablespoon salt
⅓ cup non-fat dry milk crystals

Dissolve the yeast in the lukewarm water. Stir in the butter and JIF peanut butter. Beat until smooth. Add the remaining ingredients and stir until a stiff dough is formed. Knead dough on a lightly floured board until smooth and elastic. Let rise in a warm place until double in bulk. Punch down dough and cut into 36 pieces. Shape balls into smooth rounds by pinching down dough underneath the ball. Place balls side by side in a single layer in 2 greased 13 × 9 × 2-inch baking pans. Let rise again until double in bulk. Bake in a preheated moderate oven (375° F.) for 20 to 25 minutes or until richly browned.

*Makes 3 dozen rolls*


## PEANUT BUTTER APPLE MUFFINS

2 cups sifted all-purpose flour
4 teaspoons baking powder
¾ teaspoon salt
½ teaspoon cinnamon
¼ teaspoon nutmeg
¼ cup shortening
¼ cup *Jif* creamy peanut butter
¼ cup sugar
1 egg
1 cup milk
¾ cup chopped raw apple
Sugar and cinnamon to taste

Sift the flour with the baking powder, salt, cinnamon, and nutmeg and set aside. Cream the shortening and JIF peanut butter with the sugar, beating until light and fluffy. Add the egg and beat well. Stir in the milk and chopped apple. Add the flour mixture and stir just enough to moisten the dry ingredients. Fill greased muffin tins two-thirds full. Sprinkle the top of the muffin batter with about 2 tablespoons of sugar mixed with ¼ teaspoon of cinnamon. Bake in a hot oven (400° F.) for 20 to 25 minutes.

*Makes 15 to 18 2-inch muffins*

## PEANUT-BACON CORN MUFFINS

1 12-ounce package corn muffin mix
½ cup Jif creamy peanut butter
1 tablespoon ready-to-use crumbled bacon or bacon-flavored soybean bits
1 egg
⅔ cup milk

Place the corn muffin mix in a bowl. Add the JIF peanut butter and cut in with a pastry blender or two knives. Toss in the crumbled bacon. Add the egg and milk; blend only until the dry ingredients are thoroughly moistened. Fill 12 greased 2½-inch (medium-sized) muffin cups two-thirds full. Bake in a preheated hot oven (400° F.) for about 15 minutes or until golden brown.

*Makes 12*

## PEANUT BUTTER FRUIT BASKETS

| | |
|---|---|
| 1 package (13¾ ounces) hot roll mix | ⅓ cup chopped salted peanuts |
| ½ cup *Jif* creamy peanut butter | 1 tablespoon prune juice |
| ½ cup brown sugar, firmly packed | 3 tablespoons melted butter (about) |
| 1 cup pitted cooked prunes | 1 cup confectioners' sugar |
| 1½ teaspoons cinnamon | 1 teaspoon vanilla |
| | 2 tablespoons milk |

Prepare the hot roll mix according to package directions. Let rise until double in bulk. While dough is rising, combine the JIF peanut butter, brown sugar, prunes, cinnamon, peanuts and prune juice. Beat until filling is smooth and creamy. Punch down dough and roll out on a lightly floured board to a ⅛-inch thickness. Cut out 18 4-inch rounds. Place 1 tablespoon of filling on each round. Pinch dough up around filling and place dough, pinched side up, into greased muffin pans. Brush tops with melted butter. Let rise in a warm place until double in bulk. Bake in a preheated moderate oven (350° F.) for 12 to 15 minutes. Cool 10 minutes. Combine the sugar, vanilla and milk. Beat well until smooth. Spoon glaze over top of fruit baskets.

*Makes 18*

# Cookies

## PEANUT BUTTER WHEAT DROPS

1½ cups sifted all-purpose flour
¾ teaspoon baking soda
½ teaspoon baking powder
½ teaspoon salt
½ cup *Jif* creamy peanut butter
½ cup butter
1¼ cups firmly packed brown sugar
1 egg, unbeaten
2 tablespoons milk
1½ cups crisp whole-wheat flakes
¾ cup salted peanuts

Sift the flour once, measure. Add the baking soda, baking powder and salt, and sift again. In a separate bowl, cream JIF peanut butter and butter together. Add the sugar gradually, and cream together until light and fluffy. Add the egg and beat well. Add the sifted dry ingredients alternately with the milk, mixing well after each addition. Stir in the cereal and peanuts. Drop by teaspoonfuls onto a greased baking sheet. Bake in a moderate oven (375° F.) for about 8 minutes or until golden brown.

*Makes about 4 dozen*

# SCOTTISH PEANUT BUTTER SCONES WITH LEMON CURD

2 cups all-purpose flour
2½ teaspoons baking powder
½ teaspoon salt
2 tablespoons sugar
¼ cup *Jif* creamy peanut butter
½ cup milk
1 egg, well beaten

**LEMON CURD**
¼ cup butter or margarine
1 tablespoon cornstarch
½ cup lemon juice
Grated rind of 1 lemon
1 cup sugar
1 egg, well beaten

In a large bowl, combine the flour, baking powder, salt and sugar. Cut in the JIF peanut butter until particles are very fine. Combine the milk and egg and add all at once to the dry ingredients. Stir until a soft dough is formed. Knead a few times on a lightly floured board until smooth. Roll out to a ½-inch thickness. Cut into 18 triangles. Bake in a preheated hot oven (450° F.) for 10 to 12 minutes or until lightly browned. To prepare lemon curd, melt the butter and stir in the cornstarch. Stir in the lemon juice, rind and sugar. Beat in the egg. Cook over a low heat, stirring constantly, until the sauce thickens. Serve spread while warm with warm scones.

*Makes 18*

# Cookies

## PEANUT HEALTH MUNCHIES

- 1 cup butter or margarine
- 1 cup *Jif* creamy peanut butter
- 2 cups firmly packed brown sugar
- 2 eggs
- 1 teaspoon vanilla
- 1 teaspoon ground nutmeg
- 2½ cups sifted all-purpose flour
- 1½ teaspoons baking soda
- 1 jar (2¾ ounces) sesame seeds
- 1 egg white, slightly beaten
- 2 cups wheat germ

Cream the butter until light and fluffy. Stir in the JIF peanut butter, brown sugar, eggs, vanilla and nutmeg. Stir in the flour, baking soda and sesame seeds. Shape the mixture into 1-inch balls. Dip the balls into the egg white, then roll in the wheat germ. Place on greased baking sheets, 2 inches apart. Bake in a preheated moderate oven (375° F.) for 8 to 10 minutes. Cool cookies on a rack.

*Makes about 7 dozen*

## PEANUT-APPLE TEARDROPS

- 2 cups sifted all-purpose flour
- ½ teaspoon salt
- ½ teaspoon cinnamon
- ½ teaspoon nutmeg
- ½ teaspoon cloves
- 1 cup chopped raisins
- ½ cup *Jif* creamy peanut butter
- ½ cup shortening
- 1 cup sugar
- 1 teaspoon baking soda
- 1 cup applesauce
- 1 egg, well beaten

Sift the flour, measure. Add the salt, cinnamon, nutmeg and cloves and sift again. Mix in the raisins. In a separate large bowl, cream the JIF peanut butter and shortening together. Add the sugar gradually and cream until light and fluffy. Mix the baking soda with the applesauce and add with the beaten egg to the creamed mixture. Stir in the flour mixture, mixing only enough to blend. Drop by teaspoonfuls onto a greased baking sheet. Bake in a moderate oven (375° F.) for about 15 minutes.

*Makes 4 to 5 dozen*

## PERSIAN PEANUT DROPS

| | |
|---|---|
| 1 cup unsifted confectioners' sugar | ¾ cup Jif creamy peanut butter |
| ⅛ teaspoon salt | ¾ cup chopped dates |
| 3 egg whites, unbeaten | ½ cup flaked coconut |
| 1 teaspoon vanilla | |

Add the sugar and salt to the egg whites and stir until the sugar is dissolved. Add the remaining ingredients. Mix well. Drop by teaspoonfuls onto a greased baking sheet. Bake in a moderate oven (350° F.) for 15 minutes.

*Makes 3 to 3½ dozen*

## PROTEIN PEANUT BUTTER BREAKFAST COOKIES

| | |
|---|---|
| 1 package (15 ounces) raisins | 3 eggs |
| ½ cup sugar | 1 teaspoon vanilla |
| ½ cup water | 1 cup chopped raw or salted peanuts |
| ½ cup (1 stick) butter or margarine | 3 cups sifted all-purpose flour |
| ½ cup Jif creamy peanut butter | 1 cup wheat germ |
| 1 package (1 pound) dark brown sugar | 1 teaspoon baking soda |
| | 1 teaspoon salt |
| | 2 teaspoons nutmeg |

In a saucepan, combine the raisins, sugar and water. Simmer for 3 minutes or until liquid is almost absorbed. Cool and set aside. Cream together the butter and JIF peanut butter until light and fluffy. Beat in the sugar. Beat in the eggs one at a time until smooth. Stir in the vanilla, peanuts and raisins. Stir in the remaining ingredients and mix until well blended. Drop by heaping teaspoonfuls onto a greased baking sheet. Bake in a preheated moderate oven (350° F.) for 10 to 12 minutes or until lightly browned. Cool cookies on a rack. Store in an air-tight container in a cool dry place.

*Makes 72 2-inch cookies*

## PEANUT BARS

4 egg yolks, well beaten
1 cup sugar
2 teaspoons baking powder
3 tablespoons water
1 teaspoon vanilla
3 cups coarse, dry breadcrumbs
1 cup chopped peanuts
4 egg whites, stiffly beaten

Beat the egg yolks until thick and lemon-colored. Blend in the sugar. Add the baking powder, water and vanilla. Add the dry breadcrumbs and chopped peanuts. Fold in the stiffly beaten egg whites. Turn mixture into an oblong well-greased 2-quart baking pan. Bake in a moderate oven (350° F.) for 35 minutes. Cut into 18 equal servings.
*Makes 18*

## KENLEY'S CINNAMON CRINKLES

¾ cup sifted all-purpose flour
1 teaspoon baking soda
¼ teaspoon salt
½ teaspoon cinnamon
½ cup Jif creamy peanut butter
¼ cup shortening
½ cup firmly packed brown sugar
½ cup granulated sugar
1 egg
1 teaspoon vanilla

Sift the flour with the baking soda, salt and cinnamon. In a separate large bowl, mix the JIF peanut butter with the shortening. Add the sugars and cream until light and fluffy. Beat in the egg and vanilla. Stir in the sifted dry ingredients. Chill for 10 minutes.

"Shoot" from a cookie gun onto aluminum baking sheets spacing the cookies 2 inches apart. Bake in a moderate oven (375° F.) for 8 to 10 minutes.

*Makes 5 to 6 dozen medium-thick cookies*

## PEANUT BUTTER DAISY CUPS

- ¾ cup vegetable shortening
- 1 cup sugar
- ½ cup Jif creamy peanut butter
- 1 egg
- 2 cups unsifted all-purpose flour
- 1 teaspoon vanilla
- 1 package (11 ounces) chocolate-covered peanut butter cups (small size)

Cream the shortening until fluffy. Stir in the sugar, JIF peanut butter and egg. Stir in the flour and then the vanilla. Knead the dough a few times on a floured board to make a smooth ball. Roll out two-thirds of the dough into a ¼-inch thickness. Cut into forty 2-inch rounds using a cookie cutter or a glass. Place the rounds on a greased baking sheet. Top with the peanut butter cups placed upside down. Pinch off pea-size pieces of the remaining dough. Roll each piece into a rope 2 inches long. Place two ropes in a crisscross on top of each peanut butter cup. Bake in a preheated moderate oven (350° F.) for 12 to 15 minutes or until cookies are lightly browned. Cool on the cookie sheet; then store in an air-tight container in dry place.

*Makes 40*

## ITALIAN PEANUT COOKIES

2½ cups sifted all-purpose flour
1¼ cups sifted confectioners' sugar
1½ teaspoons baking powder
3 tablespoons cocoa
⅓ cup *Jif* creamy peanut butter
1 cup salted peanuts
1 egg
1 cup evaporated milk

**ORANGE RUM FROSTING**
1½ cups sifted confectioners' sugar
2 tablespoons melted butter
3 tablespoons rum
2 teaspoons grated orange rind

In a large bowl, combine the flour, sugar, baking powder and cocoa. Cut in the JIF peanut butter until the mixture is like coarse cornmeal. Stir in the peanuts. Beat the egg and milk together. Add the liquid all at once to the dry ingredients. Stir until blended. Drop the mixture by teaspoonfuls onto a greased baking sheet. Bake in a preheated moderate oven (350° F.) for 10 to 12 minutes or until firm to the touch. Cool cookies on a rack. Combine all the frosting ingredients and stir until well blended and smooth. When the cookies are almost cool, spoon the Orange Rum Frosting over the tops.

*Makes 3 dozen*

# THE ALL-HOMEMADE PEANUT BUTTER SQUARES

¾ cup *Jif* creamy peanut butter
⅓ cup butter or margarine
2 cups sugar
1 cup firmly packed brown sugar
4 eggs
1½ teaspoons vanilla
3 cups sifted all-purpose flour
1 tablespoon baking powder
1 teaspoon salt
¼ cup chopped peanuts

**TOPPING**
1½ cups firmly packed brown sugar
½ cup butter or margarine
¼ cup milk
1 tablespoon honey
1 cup chopped peanuts

Cream the JIF peanut butter, butter and sugars in a large bowl. Add the eggs and vanilla and beat until well blended. Sift together the dry ingredients. Add to the creamed mixture with the chopped peanuts. Mix until smooth. Spread batter evenly in a greased 13 × 9 × 2-inch pan. Bake in a preheated moderate oven (350° F.) for 35 minutes. For topping: combine in a saucepan the sugar, butter, milk and honey. Bring to a boil and cook slowly for 10 minutes. Remove from heat and add the peanuts. Let cool and spread on the warm cake. Cut into squares.

*Makes about 28 squares*

## BRIDE'S FINGERS

¼ cup vegetable shortening
½ cup honey
½ cup sugar
½ cup *Jif* crunchy peanut butter
1 egg
1¾ cups sifted all-purpose flour
½ teaspoon baking powder
½ teaspoon baking soda
¼ teaspoon salt
Sugar mixed with cinnamon for topping

Cream the shortening and stir in the honey and sugar. Stir in the JIF peanut butter and egg. Mix the dry ingredients together and stir into the batter until a stiff dough is formed. With floured hands, pinch off pieces of dough about the size of a walnut. Shape into finger-length rolls about 4 inches long and half a width of one finger. Place on greased baking sheets. Bake in a preheated hot oven (400° F.) for 8 to 10 minutes. Cool for 5 minutes on the baking sheets. Roll in sugar mixed with cinnamon until well coated on all sides.
*Makes 6 dozen*

## ORANGE PEANUT RUMMIES

½ cup butter or margarine
1 cup firmly packed brown sugar
1 egg
½ cup *Jif* creamy peanut butter
½ cup sifted all-purpose flour
1 cup quick-cooking oatmeal
½ teaspoon baking soda
¼ teaspoon salt
½ cup chopped unsalted peanuts
Rind and juice of 1 large orange
1 teaspoon rum extract

Cream the butter until light and fluffy. Stir in the brown sugar, egg and JIF peanut butter. Stir in the flour, oatmeal, baking soda, salt, peanuts and orange rind. Spread the batter evenly in a greased 9-inch-square baking pan. Bake in a preheated moderate oven (350° F.) for 30 to 35 minutes or until firm. Remove from oven. Mix together the orange juice and rum extract. Brush the mixture over the warm cookie dough until all the liquid is absorbed. Cool in pan. Cut into 36 squares.

*Makes 3 dozen*

## OATMEAL REFRIGERATOR COOKIES

1¾ cups sifted all-purpose flour
2 teaspoons baking soda
¾ teaspoon salt
½ cup *Jif* creamy peanut butter
½ cup butter
2 cups firmly packed brown sugar
1 teaspoon vanilla
2 eggs
1½ cups rolled oats
½ cup chopped peanuts

Sift the flour with the baking soda and salt and set aside. In a large bowl, cream together the JIF peanut butter and butter. Add the sugar gradually and cream together until light and fluffy. Add the vanilla and eggs. Beat well. Stir in the sifted flour mixture. Then add the rolled oats and chopped nuts. Shape into rolls about 2 inches in diameter. Wrap in plastic food wrap, waxed paper or foil. Chill in the refrigerator. When ready to bake, cut into ⅛-inch-thick slices. Place on a greased baking sheet and bake in a moderate oven (350° F.) for about 15 minutes.

*Makes 6 to 6½ dozen*

## CHATTAHOOCHEE CRUNCHIES

2 cups sugar
¼ cup cocoa
½ cup milk
4 tablespoons butter or margarine
½ cup *Jif* creamy peanut butter
Dash salt
2 cups quick-cooking oatmeal
1 cup shredded coconut
1 teaspoon vanilla

In a saucepan, combine the sugar, cocoa, milk and butter. Bring mixture to a boil and cook 1 minute, stirring constantly. Remove from heat. Add the JIF peanut butter, salt, oatmeal, coconut and vanilla. Mix well. Drop by teaspoonfuls onto waxed paper, keeping mixture over hot water while dropping. Cool.
*Makes 2½ dozen*

## PEANUT-BANANA OATMEAL SPECIALS

1½ cups sifted all-purpose flour
½ teaspoon baking powder
¾ teaspoon salt
¾ teaspoon cinnamon
¼ teaspoon nutmeg
½ cup margarine
½ cup *Jif* creamy peanut butter
1 cup sugar
1 egg
1 ripe banana, mashed
1½ cups quick-cooking oatmeal

Sift the flour, baking powder, salt, cinnamon and nutmeg together; set aside. Cream the margarine, JIF peanut butter and sugar together until light and fluffy. Beat in the egg and banana. Fold in the flour mixture and oatmeal, stirring only enough to blend. Drop by teaspoonfuls onto a greased baking sheet. Bake in a moderate oven (375° F.) for 8 to 10 minutes.

*Makes 4½ dozen*

## SUPERIOR PEANUT BUTTER COOKIES

| | |
|---|---|
| 1 cup butter or margarine | 2 eggs |
| 1 cup *Jif* creamy peanut butter | 2 cups all-purpose flour |
| | 1 teaspoon baking soda |
| 1 cup granulated sugar | 1 package (6 ounces) semisweet chocolate bits |
| 1 cup firmly packed brown sugar | |

Cream the butter and JIF peanut butter together. Gradually add the sugars. Cream until blended. Add the eggs, one at a time. Beat until smooth. Stir the flour, measure, then sift again with the baking soda into the creamed mixture. Stir in the chocolate bits. Drop by teaspoonfuls onto a greased baking sheet, then slightly flatten cookie dough with the back of a spoon. Bake in a moderately slow oven (325° F.) for 15 minutes.

*Makes 6 dozen 2-inch cookies*

## PEANUT MARSHMALLOW SQUARES

2 tablespoons butter or margarine
¼ cup *Jif* creamy peanut butter
8 ounces large marshmallows (about 32)
4 cups dry oat cereal

1 cup salted peanuts

**TOPPING**
3 squares (3 ounces) semisweet chocolate
3 tablespoons *Jif* creamy peanut butter

In a saucepan, combine the butter, ¼ cup of JIF peanut butter and the marshmallows. Cook over low heat until the marshmallows are melted and the mixture is smooth. Fold in the dry cereal and peanuts. Spread the mixture with buttered fingers evenly into a buttered 9 × 9 × 2-inch pan. In a saucepan, melt the chocolate and 3 tablespoons JIF peanut butter, stirring until the mixture is smooth. Spread this topping mixture over the cereal mixture. Chill until set. Cut into 1½-inch squares with a sharp knife.

*Makes 3 dozen 1½-inch squares*

## MAHO BAY MOUNDS

1 cup *Jif* creamy peanut butter
2 packages (6 ounces each) semisweet chocolate bits

½ cup flaked coconut
½ cup raisins
1½ cups salted peanuts
About 36 graham crackers
Additional coconut

In a saucepan, melt the JIF peanut butter and chocolate over very low heat, stirring until the mixture is smooth. Fold in the coconut, raisins and peanuts. Spoon mixture on top of graham crackers. Sprinkle with additional coconut. Chill until set.

*Makes about 3 dozen*

## MARBLED PEANUT BUTTER BROWNIES

2 cups sifted all-purpose flour
2 teaspoons baking powder
½ teaspoon salt
½ cup *Jif* creamy or crunchy peanut butter
⅓ cup butter or margarine
1 cup sugar
1 cup firmly packed light brown sugar
3 eggs
1 teaspoon vanilla
½ cup chocolate bits, melted over hot water

Sift the flour, baking powder and salt together. Cream the JIF peanut butter and butter together until soft and fluffy. Gradually blend in the sugars. Beat in the eggs one at a time. Stir in the vanilla. Add flour mixture and beat until smooth and well blended. Batter will be stiff. Turn into a greased and floured 9 × 13 × 2-inch pan. Drop teaspoonfuls of melted chocolate over top of batter. With the tip of a knife, swirl chocolate into batter to create marbled effect. Bake in a preheated moderate oven (350° F.) for 30 minutes. Cool in pan. Cut into bars of desired size.

*Makes about 20 to 24 bars*

## PEANUT BUTTER CRISPS

4 cups cornflakes
1 cup soft butter or margarine
½ cup *Jif* creamy or crunchy peanut butter
½ cup granulated sugar
½ cup firmly packed brown sugar
1 egg
1 teaspoon vanilla
1⅓ cups sifted all-purpose flour
Salted peanuts

Crush the cornflakes into fine crumbs and set aside. In a large bowl, blend the butter and JIF peanut butter together. Blend in the sugars. Add the egg and vanilla. Beat well. Stir in the flour, mixing thoroughly. Shape mixture into small balls; roll in the cornflake crumbs. Place on greased baking sheets. Press one peanut into each ball. Bake in a moderate oven (350° F.) for about 15 minutes.

*Makes about 4 dozen 2-inch cookies*

## CRUNCHY PEANUT COOKIES

½ cup butter or margarine
½ cup *Jif* creamy or crunchy peanut butter
¾ cup sugar
2 eggs
½ cup milk
2 cups unsifted all-purpose flour
3 teaspoons baking powder
½ teaspoon salt
1 cup raisins
1 cup salted peanuts
3 cups cornflakes

In a large bowl, cream the butter and JIF peanut butter together. Stir in the sugar, eggs and milk. Beat in the flour, baking powder and salt until smooth. Fold in the raisins, peanuts and cornflakes. Drop by heaping teaspoonfuls onto greased baking sheets. Bake in a preheated moderate oven (350° F.) for 15 minutes or until lightly browned. Cool cookies on a rack. To retain crispness store in an air-tight container in a cool, dry place.

*Makes about 60 2-inch cookies*

## PEANUT-CHOCOLATE SANDWICH COOKIES

3 cups sifted all-purpose flour
¼ teaspoon salt
⅓ cup sugar
6 tablespoons butter or margarine
½ cup *Jif* creamy peanut butter
1 egg yolk
1 teaspoon grated orange rind
½ cup heavy cream

FILLING
4 ounces semisweet chocolate, melted
⅓ cup *Jif* creamy peanut butter
¼ cup sifted confectioners' sugar

TOPPING
2 squares (2 ounces) semisweet chocolate, melted
2 tablespoons butter or margarine

In a large bowl, combine the flour, salt and sugar. Add the butter, JIF peanut butter, egg yolk, orange rind and heavy cream. Stir until a stiff dough cleans the bowl. Knead dough a few times until a smooth ball forms. Roll out on a lightly floured board to a ⅛-inch thickness. Cut dough with a cookie cutter into 80 2-inch rounds. Place rounds on an ungreased baking sheet.

Bake in a preheated moderate oven (375° F.) for 10 to 12 minutes or until lightly browned. Cool cookies on a rack. In a small saucepan, melt the chocolate for filling. Stir in the JIF peanut butter and sugar. Spread mixture on 40 of the cookies. Top with the remaining cookies. In a small saucepan, melt the topping chocolate. Stir in the butter. Place mixture in a pastry bag fitted with a writing tip. Decorate cookies with crisscross designs of chocolate.

*Makes 40*

# PEANUT-DATE MERINGUE BALLS

| | |
|---|---|
| 1 cup roasted peanuts, chopped | 2 egg whites, room temperature |
| 1 cup dates, chopped fine | ⅛ teaspoon salt |
| ½ teaspoon vanilla | ⅔ cup sugar |

Combine the nuts, dates and vanilla. Form into ¾-inch balls. Beat the egg whites and salt until stiff. Add the sugar one tablespoon at a time while blending meringue at high speed in an electric mixer. Drop balls of the nut mixture into the meringue one at a time, using a teaspoon to roll nut balls around in meringue so they are well coated. Place on a slightly greased baking sheet. Bake in a preheated very slow oven (250° F.) for 30 minutes. Store in an air-tight container in a cool, dry place.

*Makes about 30*

## PEANUT BUTTER-DATE REFRIGERATOR COOKIES

4 cups sifted all-purpose flour
1 teaspoon baking powder
¼ teaspoon baking soda
1 teaspoon salt
1 teaspoon cinnamon
½ teaspoon nutmeg
½ cup *Jif* creamy peanut butter
1 cup margarine
1 cup firmly packed brown sugar
⅔ cup granulated sugar
2 eggs
1 cup chopped dates
1 tablespoon flour

Sift 4 cups of flour with the baking powder, baking soda, salt and spices. Set aside. In a separate large bowl, cream the JIF peanut butter and margarine together. Gradually stir in the sugars, beating until light and fluffy. Add the eggs and beat well. Gradually add the flour mixture, mixing to blend. Mix in the dates, which have been sprinkled with 1 tablespoon of additional flour. Shape into 4 rolls about 8 inches long. Wrap in plastic food wrap, waxed paper or foil. Chill thoroughly in the refrigerator. (Unbaked cookie dough may be stored in the refrigerator for several weeks.) When ready to bake, cut into thin slices. Bake on an ungreased baking sheet in a moderately hot oven (400° F.) for 5 to 8 minutes.

*Makes 6½ dozen*

## PEANUT BUTTER LEMON ICE-BOX COOKIES

| | |
|---|---|
| 2 cups all-purpose flour | 1 cup firmly packed light brown sugar |
| 1 teaspoon baking soda | 1 egg |
| ½ teaspoon salt | 1 tablespoon grated lemon rind |
| 1 cup *Jif* creamy peanut butter | 2 tablespoons lemon juice |
| 1 cup butter or margarine | |

Sift the flour, measure. Add the baking soda and salt and sift again. In a separate bowl, combine the JIF peanut butter and margarine and stir to blend. Add the sugar gradually, beating until light and fluffy. Beat in the egg, lemon rind and lemon juice. Stir in the flour mixture, mixing just enough to blend. Shape into two 12-inch-long rolls about 1½ inches in diameter. Wrap in plastic food wrap, waxed paper or foil. Chill thoroughly (overnight, if possible). When ready to bake, cut into ⅛-inch-thick slices. Bake on ungreased baking sheets in a preheated moderate oven (375° F.) for 8 to 10 minutes. Cool on the baking sheets for about 2 minutes before removing to a wire rack to finish the cooling process. Store in an air-tight container in a cool, dry place.

*Makes 9 dozen*

## PEANUT BRITTLE KISSES

| | |
|---|---|
| 2 egg whites | 1 cup crushed peanut brittle |
| ⅛ teaspoon salt | |
| ½ cup sugar | |

Beat the egg whites with the salt until foamy. Gradually add the sugar, beating until the egg whites are very stiff. Fold in the peanut brittle. Drop by teaspoonfuls onto a greased baking sheet. Bake in a slow oven (275° F.) for about 40 minutes or until lightly browned and dry on the surface.

*Makes about 3 dozen*

## HONEY PEANUT ICE-BOX SLICES

4 cups sifted all-purpose flour
1 teaspoon baking soda
½ teaspoon salt
1 teaspoon cinnamon
1 cup Jif creamy peanut butter
½ cup butter or margarine
½ cup sugar
1 cup honey
2 teaspoons vanilla
2 eggs, well beaten

Sift the flour, measure. Add the baking soda, salt and cinnamon and sift again. In a separate bowl, cream the JIF peanut butter and butter together. Add the sugar, honey and vanilla and continue creaming until light and fluffy. Beat in the eggs. Stir in the sifted flour mixture. Shape into four 8-inch-long rolls. Wrap in transparent food wrap, waxed paper or foil. Chill for several hours or overnight in the refrigerator. Cut into ⅛-inch-thick slices. Bake in a hot oven (400° F.) for 5 to 8 minutes.

*Makes 6 dozen*

## PEANUT BUTTER HORSESHOES

- 1½ cups all-purpose flour
- 1 teaspoon baking soda
- ¼ teaspoon salt
- ½ cup butter
- ½ cup *Jif* creamy peanut butter
- 1 cup granulated sugar
- 1 egg
- 1 teaspoon vanilla
- 1 cup sifted confectioners' sugar
- 1 tablespoon cocoa
- 1 teaspoon instant coffee

Sift the flour with the baking soda and salt. In a separate bowl, cream the butter and JIF peanut butter together until light and fluffy. Gradually beat in the granulated sugar and egg. Stir in the vanilla and flour mixture until blended and smooth. With fingers, pinch off 1-inch balls of dough. Roll each ball into a finger-length roll about 4 inches long. Shape into horseshoes on an ungreased baking sheet. Bake in a preheated moderate oven (350° F.) for 10 to 12 minutes or until lightly browned. Cool cookies on a rack. In a small bowl, combine the remaining ingredients. Roll horseshoes in the sugar mixture until well coated on all sides.

*Makes 4 dozen*


## NUT BUTTER CRESCENTS

- 1 cup unsifted all-purpose flour
- ½ cup *Jif* creamy peanut butter
- ¼ cup sugar
- 1 teaspoon vanilla
- ¼ cup butter or margarine
- 1 cup sifted confectioners' sugar
- 1 teaspoon grated orange rind

In a bowl, combine the flour, JIF peanut butter, sugar, vanilla and butter. Stir until dough cleans the bowl. Knead on a lightly floured board until smooth. Pinch off pieces the size of a large olive. Roll each piece into a rope about 3 inches long. Place ropes on an ungreased baking sheet. Turn ends down to shape crescents. Bake in a preheated moderate oven (375° F.) for 10 to 12 minutes or until cookies are lightly browned. Cool cookies on the baking sheet. In a small bowl, mix the confectioners' sugar and orange rind. Roll cooled cookies in the sugar mixture until well coated on all sides.

*Makes 30*

# CHOCOLATE PEANUT BUTTER THINS

- 2 cups all-purpose flour
- 2 teaspoons baking powder
- ½ teaspoon salt
- 1 cup sugar
- ½ cup cocoa
- ½ cup vegetable shortening
- ½ cup *Jif* crunchy peanut butter
- 2 eggs
- ⅓ cup milk
- 1 teaspoon orange extract
- Additional granulated sugar

In a large bowl, combine all ingredients except the additional granulated sugar. Stir until well blended. Shape dough into balls about the size of a walnut. Roll balls in the additional granulated sugar. Place on a greased baking sheet. Press balls of dough with the bottom of a glass until cookies are about ¼-inch thick. Bake in a preheated hot oven (400° F.) for 8 to 10 minutes. Cool on baking sheets. Store in an air-tight container in a cool, dry place.

*Makes about 4 dozen*

## PEANUT CHOCOLATE CHIP COOKIES

¼ cup butter or margarine
¼ cup vegetable shortening
2 tablespoons *Jif* creamy peanut butter
½ cup granulated sugar
½ cup firmly packed light brown sugar
1 egg
1 teaspoon vanilla
1¾ cups sifted all-purpose flour
½ teaspoon baking soda
½ teaspoon salt
1 cup salted peanuts
1 package (6 ounces) semisweet chocolate bits

In a large bowl, mix the butter, shortening and JIF peanut butter until soft and fluffy. Stir in the sugars, egg and vanilla. Stir in the dry ingredients. Fold in the peanuts and chocolate bits. Drop by teaspoonfuls, about 2 inches apart, onto ungreased baking sheets. Bake in a preheated moderate oven (375° F.) for 8 to 10 minutes, or until edges of cookies are lightly browned. Cool cookies for 5 minutes on the baking sheets before removing to a wire rack to finish the cooling process.

*Makes about 4 dozen*

# CHINESE CHOCOLATE PEANUT CLUSTERS

1 package (6 ounces) butterscotch bits
1 package (6 ounces) semisweet chocolate bits
1 cup salted peanuts
1 can (3 ounces) chow mein noodles

Pour the butterscotch bits and semisweet chocolate bits into the top of a double boiler. Place over hot water and stir until melted. Stir in the peanuts and chow mein noodles. Drop by teaspoonfuls onto waxed paper. Put in the refrigerator until firm.

*Makes about 4 dozen*

# Cakes

## PEANUT ORANGE CAKE

2 cups all-purpose flour
1 cup sugar
1 teaspoon salt
2 teaspoons baking powder
⅔ cup peanut oil
2 eggs, beaten
¾ cup orange juice

1 teaspoon vanilla

**TOPPING**
¼ cup sugar
½ cup chopped peanuts
1 teaspoon cinnamon

In a bowl, sift together the flour, sugar, salt and baking powder. Pour in the oil, beaten eggs, orange juice and vanilla. Mix until thoroughly blended. Spread evenly in a greased 9 × 13-inch pan. Combine the sugar, peanuts and cinnamon. Sprinkle topping over cake. Bake in a preheated moderate oven (375° F.) for 30 to 35 minutes. Cool in the pan on a cake rack. After cooling, keep tightly covered with foil or plastic food wrap.

*Makes approximately 15 servings*

# Cakes

## PEANUT BUTTER PICNIC CAKE

2½ cups sifted cake flour
2 teaspoons baking powder
½ teaspoon baking soda
1 teaspoon salt
½ teaspoon cinnamon
1 teaspoon allspice
1½ cups sugar

½ cup shortening, softened
½ cup *Jif* creamy peanut butter
¾ cup milk
2 eggs
1 teaspoon vanilla
1 loaf-sized package milk chocolate frosting mix

In a bowl, sift the flour with the baking powder, baking soda, salt, spices and sugar. In a separate bowl, beat the shortening and JIF peanut butter until creamy and blended. Add the sifted dry ingredients and milk. Stir to blend. Beat for 2 minutes with an electric mixer or 300 strokes by hand. Add the eggs and vanilla. Beat 1 minute more (150 strokes by hand). Grease and flour an 8-inch-square baking pan. Bake in a moderate oven (350° F.) for 60 minutes. Cool thoroughly. Frost the top with the chocolate frosting, prepared as directed.

*Makes 16 servings*

## SPICE CUPCAKES

2 cups sifted all-purpose flour
3 teaspoons baking powder
½ teaspoon salt
½ teaspoon ground cloves
½ teaspoon cinnamon

½ cup *Jif* creamy peanut butter
½ cup butter
1½ cups firmly packed brown sugar
2 eggs
1 cup milk
1 teaspoon vanilla

Sift the flour, baking powder, salt and spices together. Set aside. Cream together the JIF peanut butter and butter. Add the sugar gradually and cream together until light and fluffy. Add the eggs, one at a time, beating well after each addition. Add the sifted dry ingredients alternately with combined milk and vanilla, beginning and ending with the dry ingredients. Spoon the batter into greased and floured cupcake pans (or use paper cups to line pans). Bake in a moderate oven (350° F.) for about 25 minutes. Cool and frost.

*Makes 2 dozen medium-sized cupcakes*

# PEANUT-FLAVORED VACHERIN

**LAYERS**
6 egg whites
2 cups granulated sugar
½ cup chopped salted peanuts

**TOPPING**
1 cup (½ pint) heavy cream
1 tablespoon sugar
1 teaspoon vanilla

**FILLING**
¼ cup cornstarch
6 egg yolks
⅓ cup sugar
2 cups half and half
4 squares (4 ounces) semisweet chocolate, melted
⅓ cup Jif creamy peanut butter
¼ cup Cointreau

Leave egg whites at room temperature. In a large bowl, beat the egg whites until they hold soft peaks. Gradually beat in the sugar, ¼ cup at a time, until the mixture is stiff and glossy. Line 2 baking sheets with aluminum foil. Spread meringue mixture into two 9-inch rounds of even thickness on the foil. Sprinkle rounds with the peanuts. Bake in a preheated slow oven (275° F.) for 1 hour or until rounds are beige-colored and crisp. Cool layers on a rack. In a saucepan, mix the cornstarch, egg yolks, sugar and half and half. Stir over a low heat until the mixture starts to thicken. Add the chocolate and JIF peanut butter and stir over low heat until the mixture just starts to bubble. Remove from heat and cool. Stir in the Cointreau. Cover and chill. In a bowl, mix the heavy cream, sugar and vanilla. Whip until thick and stiff. Chill. When ready to serve, place one meringue layer, peanut side up, on a serving platter. Spread with half the chocolate mixture. Top with the second meringue layer, peanut side up. Spread the top with the remaining chocolate mixture. Spoon the whipped cream around edges of torte. Cut into wedges to serve.

*Makes 6 to 8 servings*

## PEANUT BUTTER CHOCOLATE ROLL

| | |
|---|---|
| 1 package (3¼ ounces) vanilla pudding and pie filling | ½ teaspoon cream of tartar |
| | 1 cup sugar |
| | 6 egg yolks |
| 1½ cups milk | ¼ cup cocoa |
| ⅓ cup Jif creamy peanut butter | ¼ cup all-purpose flour |
| | 1 teaspoon vanilla |
| 6 egg whites | Confectioners' sugar |

In a saucepan, mix pudding mix with 1 cup of the milk. Combine the JIF peanut butter and ½ cup of milk and beat until well blended (mixture will be lumpy). Stir the peanut butter mixture into the pudding. Cook over low heat, stirring constantly until the pudding bubbles and thickens. Cool. Beat the egg whites and cream of tartar until stiff. Gradually beat in ½ cup of the sugar, 1 tablespoon at a time, beating until stiff and glossy. Set aside. Beat the egg yolks until thick and lemon-colored. Gradually beat in the remaining sugar. Fold in the cocoa, flour and vanilla. Fold in the egg whites. Spread the mixture evenly into a 15 × 10 × 1-inch jelly-roll pan lined with aluminum foil and greased. Bake in a preheated slow oven (325° F.) for 20 to 25 minutes or until top springs back when lightly touched. Turn cake upside down on a towel that has been sprinkled with confectioners' sugar. Roll up in the towel, starting at the 10-inch side. Cool on a rack. Unroll and spread peanut butter filling on cake. Roll up again. Sprinkle roll with confectioners' sugar.

*Makes 8 to 10 servings*

## PEANUT BRITTLE CHEESECAKE

1½ cups graham cracker crumbs
1 cup finely crushed peanut brittle
⅓ cup melted butter or margarine
3 packages (8 ounces each) cream cheese
5 eggs
1 cup sugar
Grated rind of 1 orange
1 teaspoon vanilla

In a bowl, mix the crumbs, ⅓ cup of peanut brittle and the butter. Press mixture firmly into the bottom of a well-greased 8-inch spring-form pan. In a bowl, beat the cream cheese until fluffy. Beat in the eggs, sugar, orange rind and vanilla until smooth. Pour the mixture into the pan. Bake in a preheated slow oven (325° F.) for 1 hour or until firm in the center. Cool in pan. Remove sides of pan and place on a serving platter. Just before serving, sprinkle with the remaining peanut brittle.

*Makes 6 to 8 servings*

# PEANUT BUTTER MOLASSES SQUARES

1½ cups sifted all-purpose flour
½ teaspoon salt
1½ teaspoons baking powder
¼ teaspoon baking soda
1 teaspoon cinnamon
½ teaspoon cloves
⅓ cup shortening
½ cup *Jif* creamy peanut butter
½ cup sugar
½ cup unsulphured molasses
1 egg
½ cup hot water
Vanilla ice cream

Resift the flour with the salt, baking powder, baking soda and spices. In a separate bowl, cream the shortening, JIF peanut butter, and sugar together until light and fluffy. Blend in the molasses and egg. Add the sifted flour mixture alternately with the hot water, stirring only enough to blend. Turn into a greased 13 × 9 × 2-inch pan. Bake in a moderate oven (350° F.) for 25 minutes. Cool. Cut into 15 squares. Serve with a scoop of vanilla ice cream.

*Makes 15 squares*

# ATLANTA APPLE PEANUT CAKE

1¼ cups sifted all-purpose flour
1 teaspoon baking soda
1 teaspoon salt
½ teaspoon cinnamon
¼ teaspoon nutmeg
¼ teaspoon cloves
¼ cup butter or margarine
½ cup *Jif* creamy peanut butter
1 cup sugar
1 egg
1 cup applesauce

In a bowl, sift the dry ingredients together. In a separate bowl, cream together the butter, JIF peanut butter and sugar. Add the egg. Beat well. Add the sifted dry ingredients alternately with the applesauce to the creamed mixture. Pour into a greased, waxed-paper-lined pan, 8 × 8 × 2 inches. Bake in a moderate oven (350° F.) for 40 minutes or until done. Cool 5 to 10 minutes, then remove from pan to rack. Cut into squares. Frost according to personal taste.

*Makes 9 squares*

## APPLE CRUMBLE

½ cup sifted all-purpose flour
¾ cup sugar
¼ cup margarine
¼ cup Jif creamy peanut butter
4 cooking apples
½ teaspoon grated lemon rind
2 tablespoons lemon juice
2 tablespoons water
Ice cream or whipped cream

In a mixing bowl, mix the flour and ½ cup of sugar. Cut in the margarine and JIF peanut butter with a pastry blender or 2 knives until the mixture resembles coarse cornmeal. Pare, core and slice the apples. Arrange the apple slices in a 1½-quart casserole or shallow baking dish. Sprinkle with the remaining ¼ cup of sugar and the lemon rind, lemon juice and water. Cover with the peanut butter mixture. Bake in a moderate oven (350° F.) for about 45 minutes or until apples are tender. Serve warm, topped with ice cream or whipped cream.

*Makes 6 servings*

## MERINGUE SHELLS WITH CHOCOLATE-PEANUT FILLING

3 egg whites, at room temperature
¾ cup sugar
24 chocolate-covered peanut butter cups (small size)
1 cup (½ pint) heavy cream
1 tablespoon sugar
1 teaspoon orange flavoring
Grated rind of 1 small orange
½ cup chopped salted peanuts

Beat the egg whites until stiff. Gradually beat in the sugar, 1 tablespoon at a time, until stiff and glossy. Spoon the mixture into twelve ¼-cup mounds on a foil-lined baking sheet. Hollow out each mound with the back of a spoon until the meringue is shaped like a cup. Bake in a preheated very slow oven (275° F.) for 20 minutes. Remove from oven and top each meringue with two peanut butter cups. Replace in the oven and bake 20 minutes longer. Cool on the cookie sheet. When ready to serve, place meringues on serving plates. In a bowl, beat the remaining ingredients, except the nuts, until thick and fluffy. Spoon the mixture over the meringues. Top with the chopped peanuts. Serve at once.

*Makes 12*

## DOUBLE FUDGE
## PEANUT BUTTER CAKE

2 cups all-purpose flour
1½ cups sugar
1½ teaspoons baking soda
½ teaspoon salt
¼ cup vegetable shortening
¼ cup *Jif* creamy peanut butter
1½ cups buttermilk or sour milk
2 small eggs
1 teaspoon vanilla
3 squares (3 ounces) unsweetened chocolate, melted

**SAUCE**
1 package (6 ounces) semisweet chocolate pieces
2 tablespoons *Jif* creamy peanut butter
½ cup light cream
1 teaspoon grated orange rind
1 teaspoon vanilla

Combine all dry ingredients and blend. Add the shortening, JIF peanut butter, buttermilk, eggs, vanilla and chocolate. Beat with an electric mixer until smooth and well blended. Pour the batter into a greased 9 × 13 × 2-inch pan. Bake in a preheated moderate oven (350° F.) for 45 to 50 minutes or until cake tests done. Cool and cut into squares. Combine the remaining ingredients in a saucepan. Stir over low heat until the chocolate is melted and the sauce is smooth. Spoon hot sauce over cake squares.

*Makes 8 to 10 servings*

# PEANUT BUTTER ROLL WITH CRANBERRY FILLING

4 eggs
1¾ cups sugar
1 teaspoon butterscotch or maple flavoring
2 cups sifted all-purpose flour
¼ cup *Jif* creamy peanut butter
2 teaspoons baking powder
½ teaspoon salt
1 cup lukewarm milk
Confectioners' sugar

**FILLING**
1 jar (14 ounces) cranberry-orange relish

**FROSTING**
¼ cup butter or margarine
⅓ cup *Jif* creamy peanut butter
2 cups sifted confectioners' sugar
Milk

Leave eggs at room temperature. Grease a 15 × 10 × 1-inch jelly-roll pan and line with foil. Grease foil again. Beat the eggs until thick and fluffy. Gradually beat in the sugar, ¼ cup at a time, until the eggs are very thick. Beat in the flavoring. In a separate bowl, combine the flour and JIF peanut butter and cut until particles are very fine. Stir in the baking powder and salt. Fold flour mixture into the eggs. Gradually stir in the milk. Turn the batter into pan. Bake in a preheated moderate oven (375° F.) for 25 minutes or until cake is golden brown and springs back when lightly touched. Do not overbake. Turn cake upside down on a towel that has been sprinkled with confectioners' sugar. Spread cake quickly with cranberry-orange relish. Roll up starting at the 10-inch side. Place on a platter and cool. Cream the butter and JIF peanut butter. Beat in the 2 cups of confectioners' sugar. Beat in enough milk until the frosting consistency is fluffy and easy to spread. Spread frosting over the top and ends of the roll. Cut in 1-inch slices.

*Makes 10 slices*

## ALABAMA PRIZE PEANUT BUTTER CAKE

**CAKE**
- 1 cup (2 sticks) butter or margarine
- ¼ cup cocoa
- 1 cup water
- ½ cup buttermilk
- 2 eggs, well beaten
- 2 cups sugar
- 2 cups unsifted all-purpose flour
- 1 teaspoon baking soda
- 1 teaspoon vanilla

**TOPPING**
- 1½ cups *Jif* creamy peanut butter
- 1½ tablespoons peanut oil

**FROSTING**
- ½ cup (1 stick) butter or margarine
- ¼ cup cocoa
- 6 tablespoons buttermilk
- 1 package (1 pound) confectioners' sugar
- 1 teaspoon vanilla

In a saucepan, combine the butter, cocoa, water, buttermilk and eggs. Stir constantly over low heat until the mixture bubbles. In a large bowl, mix the sugar, flour and baking soda. Stir the hot mixture into the dry ingredients. Beat until smooth. Stir in the vanilla. Spread the mixture evenly in a greased and floured 9 × 13 × 2-inch baking pan. Bake in a preheated moderate oven (350° F.) for 25 minutes or until puffed and firm to the touch in the center. In a bowl, mix the JIF peanut butter evenly over the cooled cake. In a saucepan, heat the butter, cocoa and buttermilk until bubbly. Place the sugar in a large bowl. Beat in the hot mixture. Beat until smooth. Stir in the vanilla. Spread mixture evenly over peanut topping. Cut into squares.

*Makes approximately 15 servings*

## PEANUT BUTTER COCONUT CAKE

**CAKE**
- 2¼ cups unsifted cake flour
- 1½ cups sugar
- ½ teaspoon salt
- 1 tablespoon baking powder
- ¼ cup *Jif* creamy peanut butter
- ¼ cup vegetable shortening
- 1 cup milk
- 2 teaspoons rum, vanilla, lemon or orange flavoring
- 2 eggs
- 1 can (3½ ounces) flaked coconut

**TOPPING**
- 3 cups confectioners' sugar
- ¼ cup orange juice
- Grated rind of 1 orange

In a large bowl, place the flour, sugar, salt, baking powder, JIF peanut butter, shortening, milk, rum flavoring and eggs. Beat with an electric mixer until smooth. Fold in the coconut. Spread batter evenly in a greased and floured 9 × 13 × 2-inch baking pan. Bake in a preheated moderate oven (350° F.) for 30 to 35 minutes or until firm to the touch in the center. Cool cake in pan. In a bowl, mix the confectioners' sugar, orange rind and juice. Spread the mixture over cake. Let dry at room temperature. Cut into squares.

*Makes approximately 15 servings*

## PEANUT BUTTER CARROT DELIGHT

**CAKE**
1½ cups peanut oil
2 cups sugar
5 eggs
½ cup orange juice
½ cup *Jif* creamy peanut butter
2 cups grated raw carrots (about 4 large)
1 cup raisins
3¾ cups unsifted all-purpose flour
3 teaspoons baking soda
6 teaspoons baking powder

**FROSTING**
1 can (16½ ounces) vanilla frosting
⅓ cup *Jif* creamy peanut butter
Grated rind of 1 orange

In a large bowl, mix the oil, sugar and eggs with an electric mixer until well blended and fluffy. Stir in the orange juice, JIF peanut butter, carrots and raisins. Stir in the flour, baking soda and baking powder. Pour mixture into a greased and floured 10 × 4-inch tube pan. Bake in a preheated moderate oven (350° F.) for 1 hour and 20 minutes or until cake is puffed and brown. After removing from pan, cool cake on a cake rack. In a bowl, mix the frosting, JIF peanut butter and orange rind. Spread frosting over the top and sides of cake. Cut in thin slices to serve.

*Makes 12 to 16 servings.*

## PEANUTTY BANANA CAKE

½ cup shortening
1 cup sugar
2 eggs
¾ cup milk
1 cup mashed ripe bananas

2½ cups all-purpose flour
2½ teaspoons baking powder
½ teaspoon salt
¾ cup chopped peanuts

In a large bowl, cream the shortening and sugar until light and fluffy. Beat in the eggs. Stir in the milk and bananas. In a separate bowl, sift the flour, baking powder and salt. Stir the peanuts into the dry ingredients. Stir the dry ingredients into the cake batter. Beat until smooth and well blended. Pour batter into 2 greased and floured 8-inch layer-cake pans. Bake in a preheated moderate oven (350° F.) for 30 to 35 minutes. Cool in pans for 5 minutes, then loosen edges and cool layers on a rack. When cool, spread frosting of your choice between layers and over sides and top of cake.

*Makes 6 to 8 servings*

## PARTY LAYER CAKE

2 cups sifted cake flour
2 teaspoons baking powder
½ teaspoon baking soda
1 teaspoon salt
½ cup *Jif* creamy peanut butter

¼ cup butter
1½ cups firmly packed brown sugar
2 eggs
⅔ cup milk
1 teaspoon vanilla

Sift together the flour, baking powder, baking soda and salt. Set aside. In a large bowl, cream together the JIF peanut butter and butter. Add the brown sugar gradually and cream together until light and fluffy. Add the eggs and beat well. Add the sifted dry ingredients alternately with the combined milk and vanilla, beginning and ending with the dry ingredients. Beat well after each addition. Pour batter into 2 greased and floured 8-inch pans. Bake in a moderate oven (350° F.) for about 30 minutes. When cool, spread frosting of your choice between layers and over sides and top of cake.

*Makes 6 to 8 servings*

## PEANUT BUTTER CAKE

| | |
|---|---|
| ¾ cup *Jif* creamy peanut butter | 3 eggs |
| ½ cup vegetable shortening | 3 cups all-purpose flour |
| 1½ teaspoons vanilla | 3 teaspoons baking powder |
| 2¼ cups firmly packed light brown sugar | ½ teaspoon salt |
| | 1¼ cups milk |

In a large bowl, cream together the JIF peanut butter, shortening and vanilla. Beat in the sugar. Add eggs, one at a time, beating after each addition. In another bowl, mix the flour, baking powder and salt. Alternately add the dry ingredients and milk to the peanut butter mixture, beginning and ending with the dry ingredients. Bake in 3 greased and floured 9-inch layer-cake pans. Bake in a preheated moderate oven (350° F.) for 30 to 35 minutes or until cake shrinks from sides of pan. Cool layers on a rack and spread frosting of your choice between layers and over sides and top of cake.

*Makes 8 to 10 servings*

# Desserts

## PEANUT BUTTER BROWN BETTY

4 large cooking apples, peeled, cored and sliced
½ cup raisins
1 teaspoon cinnamon
½ cup sugar
2 tablespoons lemon juice
½ cup butter or margarine
⅓ cup firmly packed brown sugar
⅓ cup *Jif* creamy peanut butter
4 cups soft breadcrumbs
Thick cream

Mix the apples, raisins, cinnamon, sugar and lemon juice together. Pour the mixture into a 2-quart casserole. In a skillet, melt the butter and stir in the brown sugar and JIF peanut butter. Stir until the mixture is well blended. Stir in the breadcrumbs until all particles are blended. Sprinkle mixture evenly over apples. Bake in a preheated moderate oven (350° F.) for 40 to 45 minutes or until apples are easily pierced and the top is crisp. Serve warm in small bowls topped with thick cream.

*Makes 6 servings*

## CREAMY PEANUT BUTTER MOLD

2 packages (6 ounces each) orange gelatin
1½ cups boiling water
3 cups (1½ pints) sour cream
1 cup *Jif* crunchy peanut butter
1 teaspoon ground cardamom or mace
1 cup heavy cream, whipped
Additional whipped cream, sweetened
Peanuts

In a saucepan, dissolve the gelatin in the boiling water. In a bowl, stir the sour cream gradually into the JIF peanut butter. Gradually beat in the gelatin mixture and cardamom. Chill until the mixture thickens slightly. Fold in the whipped cream. Pour mixture into a 2-quart mold. Chill until firm. Dip for a few seconds in hot water. Unmold and serve garnished with rosettes of additional sweetened whipped cream sprinkled with peanuts.

*Serving suggestion:* If desired, fill a 1½-quart mold and pour the remaining mixture into six ½-cup molds. Chill until firm. Unmold and serve the large mold surrounded with small molds. Garnish with rosettes of whipped cream and peanuts.

*Makes 10 servings*

# Desserts

## CHILLED PEANUT BUTTER SOUFFLÉ

- 3 envelopes unflavored gelatin
- 1½ cups milk
- 4 egg yolks
- 1 cup sugar
- 1 cup *Jif* creamy peanut butter
- 4 egg whites, stiffly beaten
- 2 cups (1 pint) heavy cream, whipped
- ½ teaspoon ground nutmeg
- 2 teaspoons grated orange rind
- Sweetened whipped cream

Soak the gelatin in the milk. In a saucepan, beat the egg yolks. Stir in the sugar, milk and gelatin. Stir over low heat until the mixture thickens. Do not boil. Stir in the JIF peanut butter and beat until the JIF peanut butter is smoothly blended into the custard. Chill until cold and slightly thickened. Fold in the egg whites, whipped cream, nutmeg and orange rind. Make a foil collar 2 inches high around the outer edge of a 1-quart soufflé dish. Pour in the peanut butter mixture. Chill until firm. Carefully remove foil collar and serve topped with sweetened whipped cream.

*Makes 6 to 8 servings*

## FROZEN PEANUT BUTTER PIE

- 4 ounces cream cheese
- 1 cup confectioners' sugar
- ⅓ cup *Jif* creamy peanut butter
- ½ cup milk
- 1 package (9 ounces) frozen nondairy whipped topping
- 1 9-inch graham cracker crust or regular pie crust, baked and cooled
- ¼ cup finely chopped peanuts

In a large bowl, whip the cheese until soft and fluffy. Beat in the sugar and JIF peanut butter. Slowly add the milk, blending thoroughly into mixture. Fold whipped topping into mixture. Pour into baked pie shell. Sprinkle with chopped peanuts. Freeze until firm and serve. If not used the same day, wrap in transparent food wrap after the pie is frozen. Remove from freezer about ½ hour before serving.

*Makes 6 servings*

## AUTUMN FESTIVAL FLUFF

- 1½ cups graham cracker crumbs
- ½ cup firmly packed light brown sugar
- ½ cup Jif crunchy peanut butter
- ¼ cup melted butter or margarine
- ¾ cup confectioners' sugar
- ⅓ cup Jif crunchy peanut butter
- 1 package (8 ounces) cream cheese
- ¾ cup granulated sugar
- 2 cups (1 pint) heavy cream, whipped
- 1 can (1 pound, 4 ounces) pie-sliced apples, drained
- Ground cinnamon

Combine the crumbs, brown sugar, ½ cup of JIF peanut butter, and the butter. Mix until crumbly. In another bowl, combine the confectioners' sugar and ⅓ cup of JIF peanut butter. Mix until crumbly. Mash the cream cheese and beat in the granulated sugar gradually until the mixture is very soft and creamy. Fold in the whipped cream. Sprinkle two-thirds of the graham crumb mixture over the bottom of a 9 × 13-inch pan. Press crumbs into place evenly. Spoon half of the cheese mixture over the crumbs. Carefully spread cheese into an even layer. Place apple slices evenly over the cheese. Sprinkle with cinnamon. Sprinkle two-thirds of the confectioners' sugar mixture over the apples. Top with the remaining cheese mixture, spreading cheese evenly over crumbs. Top with the remaining graham cracker crumbs and remaining confectioners' sugar mixture. Cover pan with foil and chill for 24 hours before serving. Cut into squares to serve.

*Makes about 12 servings*

## SOUR CREAM CHIFFON PIE

1 tablespoon (1 envelope) unflavored gelatin
⅔ cup cold water
2 eggs, separated
½ cup sugar
¼ teaspoon salt
⅔ cup *Jif* creamy peanut butter
1 cup sour cream
1 baked 9-inch pie shell
Sweetened whipped cream
Shaved chocolate

Soften the gelatin in the cold water. Beat the egg yolks, sugar and salt together in top of a double boiler. Stir in the gelatin and cook over boiling water, beating constantly with a rotary beater until the mixture is thick and fluffy. Remove from heat and blend in the JIF peanut butter. Beat the egg whites until stiff but not dry and fold with the sour cream into the gelatin mixture. Pour into a pie shell and chill in the refrigerator until firm. Serve topped with slightly sweetened whipped cream and shaved chocolate, if desired.

*Makes 6 to 8 servings*

# FROZEN PEANUT MOUSSE PIE

**CRUST**
2 cups graham cracker crumbs
¼ cup granulated sugar
½ cup melted butter or margarine

**FILLING**
1 package (3¼ ounces) vanilla pudding and pie filling
2 egg yolks
2 cups milk
½ cup *Jif* creamy peanut butter
¼ teaspoon ground nutmeg
¼ teaspoon ground mace
2 cups (1 pint) heavy cream, whipped

Combine the crumbs, sugar and butter. Press mixture firmly into bottom and sides of an ungreased 9-inch pie pan. Chill. In a saucepan, combine the pudding powder and egg yolks. Beat milk and JIF peanut butter together until smooth. Gradually stir the milk mixture into the pudding powder. Cook over low heat, stirring constantly, until custard thickens. Fold in the spices. Cool. Fold in the whipped cream. Pour mixture into the pie shell and freeze until firm. Remove pie from freezer 30 minutes before cutting and serving.

*Makes 6 to 8 servings*

# PEANUT BUTTER APPLE DUMPLINGS WITH LEMON SAUCE

**CRUST**
4 cups sifted all-purpose flour
5 teaspoons baking powder
1 teaspoon salt
⅓ cup Jif creamy peanut butter
½ cup butter or margarine
1½ cups milk

**FILLING**
6 cooking apples, peeled and cored whole
½ cup raisins
6 tablespoons sugar

**SAUCE**
3 tablespoons cornstarch
1 can (6 ounces) frozen concentrated lemonade, undiluted
1½ cups water
2 tablespoons butter or margarine

In a bowl, mix the flour, baking powder and salt. Cut in the JIF peanut butter and butter until crumbs are like coarse cornmeal. Stir in the milk and stir until dough cleans the bowl. Place dough on a heavily floured board and knead a few times until it is a smooth ball. Roll out on a floured board to a 12 × 18-inch oblong. Cut into six-inch squares. Place 1 apple on each square. Fill the centers with raisins and sprinkle with sugar. Bring opposite corners of dough over apples and pinch edges together. Place dumplings on a greased cookie sheet. Turn back corners on dumplings so tops of apples are exposed. Bake in a preheated moderate oven (375° F.) for 40 to 45 minutes or until apples are easily pierced. In a saucepan, mix the cornstarch and lemonade. Stir in the water and butter. Stir over low heat until the sauce bubbles and thickens. Serve dumplings hot with hot sauce spooned over them.

*Makes 6 servings*

## PEANUT BUTTER ICE CREAM BALLS

| | |
|---|---|
| 1 cup graham cracker crumbs | 2 tablespoons sugar |
| ¼ cup Jif creamy peanut butter | ¼ teaspoon cinnamon |
| | 1 quart vanilla ice cream |
| | Chocolate syrup |

Blend the graham cracker crumbs, JIF peanut butter, sugar, and cinnamon. Scoop ice cream into large balls and roll in crumb mixture until well coated. Freeze until serving time. Serve with chocolate syrup.

*Makes 6 to 8 servings*

## FROZEN PEANUT BRITTLE MOUSSE

| | |
|---|---|
| 2 envelopes unflavored gelatin | 1½ cups crushed peanut brittle |
| ½ cup strong coffee | 2 cups (1 pint) heavy cream, whipped |
| 2 cups milk | Additional crushed peanut brittle |
| ½ cup honey | |

In a saucepan, dissolve the gelatin in the coffee, stirring over low heat. Stir in the milk and honey until well blended. Chill until mixture thickens slightly. Fold in the peanut brittle and whipped cream. Pour mixture into 8 individual 1-cup mousse molds. Freeze until hard. For long-term storage, wrap each mold in foil after it is hard. Serve sprinkled with additional crushed peanut brittle.

*Makes 8 servings*


## PEANUT BUTTER ICE-BOX TORTE

2 8-inch sponge cake layers
½ cup Jif creamy peanut butter
2 cups (1 pint) heavy cream
¼ cup firmly packed light brown sugar
1 teaspoon vanilla
⅛ teaspoon salt

**FROSTING**
2 squares (2 ounces) unsweetened chocolate
2 tablespoons butter
2 cups confectioners' sugar, sifted
4 tablespoons milk

Split cake layers in two crosswise so that you have four layers. Put the JIF peanut butter in a medium-sized bowl and gradually blend in the cream. Stir in the brown sugar, vanilla and salt. Beat with a rotary beater until mixture is stiff. Put a split cake layer on a serving plate and spread with one-third of the cream. Top with another layer and repeat until all layers and cream are used. Chill for at least an hour. Then frost as follows: in a saucepan, combine the unsweetened chocolate and butter and melt over hot water. Add the confectioners' sugar and milk. Stir to blend. Frost cake with this mixture. Return to refrigerator and chill for several hours before serving.

*Makes 8 to 10 servings*

## PEANUT CREAM CONES

½ cup *Jif* creamy peanut butter
2 cups (1 pint) heavy cream
⅓ cup confectioners' sugar
8 flat-bottomed ice cream cones
3 tablespoons chopped peanuts
1 tablespoon chocolate sprinkles

In a bowl, combine the JIF peanut butter, heavy cream and sugar. Beat with a rotary egg beater until thick and fluffy. Spoon mixture into ice-cream cones. Sprinkle with peanuts and sprinkles. Place in freezer and freeze until hard. Wrap in transparent food wrap or foil and store until ready to serve.
*Makes 8*

# PEANUT BUTTER ICE-CREAM CAKE

**CAKE**
1 quart soft vanilla ice cream
1 package (18½ ounces) yellow cake mix
⅓ cup *Jif* creamy peanut butter
2 eggs
1⅓ cups water

**FROSTING**
½ cup *Jif* creamy peanut butter
¼ cup soft butter
1 teaspoon vanilla
¼ cup light cream
3 cups sifted confectioners' sugar

Line a 9-inch layer-cake pan with foil and chill in the freezer. Spread the soft ice cream evenly into the chilled layer-cake pan. Freeze. Combine the cake mix and ⅓ cup of JIF peanut butter until crumbs are like coarse cornmeal. Stir in the eggs and water. Beat until smooth. Pour batter into 2 greased and floured 9-inch layer-cake pans. Bake as directed on package. Remove from pan and cool on a rack. Blend the ½ cup of JIF peanut butter and butter until fluffy. Stir in the vanilla and cream. Gradually beat in the confectioners' sugar until frosting is fluffy and holds its peaks firmly. To assemble cake, place 1 cooled layer on a serving platter. Remove the ice-cream layer from pan using foil and invert on top of cake layer. Strip off foil. Top with second cake layer. Spread peanut butter frosting on top and sides of cake. Freeze until ready to serve. Cut while frozen, then thaw slices 30 minutes before serving. For long-term storage, freeze cake until hard. Wrap in freezer paper and seal.

*Makes 6 to 8 servings*

## GEORGIA PRIZE PEANUT REFRIGERATOR CAKE

- 1 pound soft butter
- ½ cup *Jif* creamy peanut butter
- 1 pound confectioners' sugar
- 1 package (11 ounces) social tea biscuits
- 1 cup cold strong coffee
- ¼ cup cocoa
- ½ cup chopped salted peanuts

In a bowl, cream the butter until light and fluffy. Gradually stir in the JIF peanut butter. Gradually beat in the confectioners' sugar until the mixture is soft and fluffy. Dip biscuits quickly, one by one, into the cold coffee and place 16 of them on a foil-lined cookie sheet (4 biscuits lengthwise and 4 biscuits across). Spread biscuits with one-fourth of the peanut butter mixture, spreading mixture carefully in an even layer. Sift over one-quarter of the cocoa. Repeat until you have 4 layers of biscuits. Spread remaining peanut butter mixture over the top and sides of the cake. Dust with the remaining cocoa. Sprinkle top and sides with chopped peanuts. Refrigerate for 12 hours. Slice thinly and serve while still cold.

*Makes 10 to 12 servings*

# Candy

## FIG PEANUT FUDGE

1½ cups granulated sugar
1½ cups firmly packed light brown sugar
⅔ cup evaporated milk
½ teaspoon cream of tartar
2 tablespoons light corn syrup
1 cup chopped dried figs
½ cup Jif creamy peanut butter
½ cup chopped peanuts

In a saucepan, combine the granulated sugar, brown sugar, milk, cream of tartar and corn syrup. Bring to a boil, stirring constantly, until 236° F. on a candy thermometer. Remove from heat. Cool at room temperature, without stirring, until bottom of pan is warm to the hand (150° F. on the thermemeter). Add the figs, JIF peanut butter and peanuts. Beat until mixture holds shape. Turn into a 6½ × 10-inch greased pan. Cut into squares when firm.

*Makes 2 dozen*

## PEANUT BUTTER DATEBALLS

½ cup *Jif* crunchy peanut butter
1 can (15 ounces) sweetened condensed milk
2 cups graham cracker crumbs
1 cup chopped pitted dates
½ teaspoon ground cinnamon
½ teaspoon ground cloves
Flaked coconut

Combine all ingredients, except the coconut, and knead with fingers until smooth. Shape mixture into small balls. Roll in the flaked coconut. Chill until firm. Store in an air-tight container in a cool, dry place.
*Makes about 3 dozen*


## PEANUT BUTTER PRUNE ROLL

3 tablespoons butter or margarine
2 tablespoons *Jif* creamy peanut butter
¼ cup evaporated milk
½ teaspoon vanilla
1 pound confectioners' sugar
1 cup finely chopped dried prunes
½ cup chopped peanuts

In a saucepan, melt the butter. Stir in the JIF peanut butter, milk and vanilla. Remove from heat. Add the sugar and prunes. Blend together and knead on a lightly floured board until smooth. Form into 2-inch-diameter roll. Coat with chopped peanuts. Chill until firm. Slice.
*Makes about 30 pieces*

## PEANUT BUTTER FUDGE

1 pound confectioners' sugar
1 teaspoon salt
½ cup *Jif* creamy peanut butter
4 tablespoons butter
¼ cup milk
1 teaspoon vanilla (added after mixture is removed from heat)

Place all ingredients, except vanilla, in top of a double boiler over boiling water. Beat until smooth. Remove from heat and add the vanilla; beat again. Quickly pour mixture into a 7 × 9-inch buttered baking pan. Cool. Cut into squares. Refrigerate. Remove squares from pan when fudge is thoroughly cold.
*Makes 40 to 50 pieces*

## PEANUT BUTTER PANOCHA

3 cups firmly packed light brown sugar (1 pound)
¼ teaspoon salt
½ cup milk
1 cup *Jif* crunchy peanut butter
2 teaspoons vanilla
¼ cup chopped salted peanuts

In a large saucepan, combine the brown sugar, salt and milk. Bring to a boil and boil without stirring until 238° F. on a candy thermometer. Remove from heat. Stir in the JIF peanut butter and vanilla. Stir until the mixture is well blended. Pour mixture into a buttered 8-inch-square pan. Sprinkle top with peanuts. Let stand at room temperature until mixture hardens. With a sharp knife, cut the panocha into small squares. Wrap each square in plastic food wrap or colored cellophane. Store in an air-tight container in a cool, dry place until ready to serve.

*Makes 16 2-inch squares*

## PEANUT BUTTER PRALINES

- 1 cup milk
- 2 tablespoons white vinegar
- 1 cup butter or margarine
- 2½ cups sugar
- ½ teaspoon baking soda
- 1 tablespoon vanilla
- ½ cup Jif creamy peanut butter
- 3 cups shelled roasted peanuts

In a saucepan, combine the milk, vinegar, butter and sugar. Bring to a boil and boil until 238° F. on a candy thermometer. Remove from heat. Stir in the baking soda, vanilla and JIF peanut butter. Beat until smooth. Stir in the peanuts. Drop by tablespoonfuls onto greased paper. Let stand at room temperature until hardened. Store in an air-tight container in a cool, dry place.

*Makes about 3½ pounds*

## PEANUT HEALTH CANDY

- 1 cup non-fat dry milk crystals
- 1 cup Jif creamy peanut butter
- 1 cup honey
- ½ cup toasted sesame seeds
- ½ cup wheat germ
- 1 egg white, slightly beaten
- 1½ cups finely chopped peanuts

Combine the milk crystals, JIF peanut butter, honey, sesame seeds and wheat germ. Knead with hands until a smooth ball is formed. Cut into 36 pieces. Roll each piece into a ball. Dip balls into the beaten egg white. Drain excess and roll balls in chopped peanuts. Let dry at room temperature. Store in an air-tight container in a cool, dry place.

*Makes 3 dozen*

# VANILLA PEANUT DIVINITY

⅓ cup egg whites (about 2 large)
3 cups sugar
¾ cup clear corn syrup
¾ cup hot water
1 teaspoon vanilla
1½ cups salted peanuts

Warm the egg whites to room temperature. In a saucepan, combine the sugar, syrup and hot water. Bring to a boil and boil until 238° F. on a candy thermometer. Remove from heat. Beat the egg whites at high speed with an electric mixer for 1 minute. Gradually pour in the hot syrup in a thin stream, beating constantly until candy holds its shape. Fold in the vanilla and peanuts. Drop quickly onto waxed paper using two buttered spoons. Cool until firm. Store in an air-tight container in a cool, dry place.

*Makes 3 dozen*

## CHRISTMAS PEANUT BUTTER MOONS

1 egg white
1 tablespoon cold water
¼ cup evaporated milk
1 teaspoon vanilla
⅛ teaspoon salt
½ cup *Jif* creamy peanut butter
4½ cups sifted confectioners' sugar
4 cups honey-flavored rice cereal

Mix the egg white with the water, milk, vanilla, salt and JIF peanut butter. Gradually blend in the sugar. Knead until smooth—about 5 minutes. Shape into small balls and roll in the cereal, pressing cereal into candy. Wrap individually in waxed paper or colored cellophane and store in an air-tight container in a cool, dry place.

*Makes about 5 dozen*

## CHOCOLATE PEANUT LOGS

1 pound confectioners' sugar
1 can (3½ ounces) flaked coconut
1 cup chopped salted peanuts
1 teaspoon vanilla
1½ cups graham cracker crumbs
½ cup *Jif* crunchy peanut butter
1 cup peanut oil
2 packages (6 ounces each) chocolate pieces
2 tablespoons vegetable shortening

Combine the sugar, coconut, peanuts, vanilla, crumbs, JIF peanut butter and oil. Mix well. Knead into a smooth ball. Pinch off pieces about 1¼ inches in diameter. Roll each piece with the fingers into a 2-inch log. Melt the chocolate and shortening in a pan set over hot water until smooth, being careful not to get any water into the chocolate. Keep pan over hot water. Place logs, one at a time, into chocolate and roll to coat each log evenly. Put a fork under the log, lift from chocolate and place on a piece of foil. Refrigerate until chocolate hardens. Store in an air-tight container in a cool, dry place.

*Makes 65 2-inch logs*

## APRICOT PEANUT BUTTER DROPS

1 cup dried apricots
1½ cups *Jif* creamy peanut butter
¼ cup honey
1 cup flaked coconut

Cut the apricots into small pieces with kitchen scissors or chop with a paring knife on a board. Combine the JIF peanut butter and honey. Blend. Stir in the chopped apricots. Drop by teaspoonfuls into the flaked coconut that has been spread on a paper plate or on waxed paper. Shape gently with fingertips into balls. Chill in the refrigerator until firm.

*Makes about 3 dozen drops*

## ORANGE PEANUT DIVINITY

2½ cups sugar
½ cup light corn syrup
½ cup water

2 egg whites
1 teaspoon orange extract
½ cup salted peanuts

In a saucepan, combine the sugar, corn syrup and water. Bring to a boil and boil until 238° F. on a candy thermometer. Beat the egg whites until stiff. Gradually beat in half of the syrup. Heat the remaining syrup to 250° F. on a candy thermometer. Beat gradually into the egg whites. Beat in the orange extract. Beat until mixture holds its shape. Fold in the peanuts. Spoon in mounds onto waxed paper. Cool until firm. Store in an air-tight container in a cool, dry place.

*Makes about 3 dozen*


## PEANUT FRUIT BALLS

1½ cups pitted prunes
1½ cups pitted dates
1½ cups dried apricots
1½ cups raisins
1½ cups salted peanuts

⅓ cup sugar
½ cup Jif creamy peanut butter
Additional chopped peanuts

Coarsely grind the prunes, dates, apricots, raisins and peanuts. Stir in the sugar and JIF peanut butter. Shape mixture into 1-inch balls. Roll balls in the chopped peanuts. Wrap in plastic food wrap. Store in an air-tight container in a cool, dry place.

*Makes 8 dozen*

## PEANUT-RAISIN BALLS

1½ cups salted peanuts
1½ cups raisins
2 cups flaked coconut
2 tablespoons lemon juice
¾ cup sweetened condensed milk (about)
Confectioners' sugar

Grind the peanuts, raisins and coconut. Stir in the lemon juice and enough sweetened condensed milk to hold mixture together. Shape mixture into 1-inch balls. Let stand on waxed paper until firm. Roll in confectioners' sugar, if desired.
*Makes about 4 dozen*

## PEANUT BUTTER OATS SUPREME

2 cups sugar
3 tablespoons cocoa
½ cup evaporated milk
½ cup butter
½ cup *Jif* creamy peanut butter
2 cups quick-rolled oats
1 teaspoon almond extract

In a saucepan, combine the sugar, cocoa, milk and butter. Stir over low heat until the butter melts. Simmer for 2 minutes. Add the JIF peanut butter, rolled oats and almond extract. Stir to mix well. Turn into a lightly greased 9 × 9 × 1½-inch pan. Refrigerate overnight. Cut into 1½-inch squares.
*Makes 3 dozen*

# EASY CHOCOLATE PEANUT BUTTER FUDGE

1½ cups sugar
¼ cup *Jif* creamy peanut butter
½ cup evaporated milk
1 cup marshmallow fluff
½ teaspoon salt
1 package (6 ounces) semisweet chocolate bits

In a saucepan, combine the sugar, JIF peanut butter, milk, marshmallow fluff, and salt. Cook and stir over low heat until blended. Continue cooking and stirring until the mixture comes to a full boil. Boil 5 minutes, stirring constantly. Remove from heat. Add the chocolate. Stir until chocolate is melted and blended into cooked mixture. Turn into a greased 8 × 8 × 2-inch pan. Cool. Cut into squares.

*Makes 3 dozen*

# GRAND PRIZE PEANUT BUTTER CANDY

- 1½ cups *Jif* creamy peanut butter
- 1 cup (2 sticks) butter or margarine
- 1½ cups graham cracker crumbs
- 1 package (1 pound) confectioners' sugar
- 1 package (14 ounces) caramels
- ¼ cup butter or margarine
- ¼ cup evaporated milk
- 1½ pounds salted peanuts, finely chopped

In a large saucepan, combine the JIF peanut butter and 1 cup of butter. Stir over low heat until smooth and melted. Remove from heat and stir in the graham cracker crumbs and sugar. Stir until well blended. Knead with the hands until a smooth ball forms. Divide into three pieces and shape each piece into a roll 11 inches long, about 1 inch in diameter. In a small saucepan, combine the caramels, ¼ cup butter and milk. Stir over low heat until smooth. Allow caramel to stand until cool and thick. Using a spatula, coat top half of each roll with the caramel. Roll the coated side in peanuts to cover. Repeat for remaining half of each roll. Refrigerate for several hours. Cut rolls into slices. Store in an air-tight container in a cool, dry place.

*Makes about 4½ pounds*

# Beverages

## ORANGE PEANUT NOG

2 tablespoons *Jif* creamy
   peanut butter
1 egg
2 tablespoons frozen

concentrated orange
   juice, undiluted
2 teaspoons sugar
1 cup skimmed milk
Dash nutmeg

Combine all ingredients in a bowl and beat with a rotary egg beater until smooth. Pour into a glass and serve at once. (This delicious beverage can be made in an electric blender.)
*Makes 1 serving*

## GOOD HEALTH BREAKFAST IN A GLASS

1 quart milk
2 ripe bananas
½ cup *Jif* creamy peanut
   butter

½ cup honey
½ cup wheat germ
4 eggs

Combine 1 cup of the milk and remaining ingredients in a blender and whirl at the highest speed until smooth. Pour mixture into a 2-quart pitcher. Stir in the remaining milk. Pour into glasses and serve. (This beverage may be made the night before and shaken very well just before serving.)

*Makes 4 servings*

## HOT MAPLE PEANUT DRINK

| | |
|---|---|
| 2 tablespoons *Jif* creamy peanut butter | 1 cup milk |
| 2 tablespoons maple syrup | Dash cinnamon, nutmeg |

Combine all ingredients in a saucepan and beat with a rotary egg beater until smooth. Heat, stirring constantly, until drink is steaming. Serve in a heatproof mug with a cinnamon stick stirrer.

*Makes 1 serving*

## PEANUT BUTTER MAPLE MILK SHAKE

| | |
|---|---|
| ½ cup *Jif* creamy peanut butter | 12 ice cubes, coarsely cracked |
| 1 quart skim milk | Vanilla ice cream |
| ½ cup maple syrup | |

Combine half of each ingredient except the ice cream in a blender. Whirl at top speed until smooth and well blended. Pour into glasses. Repeat using the remaining ingredients except the ice cream. Serve at once. Can be topped with a scoop of vanilla ice cream, if desired.

*Makes 6 servings*

## CHOCOLATE PEANUT BUTTER MILK SHAKE

| | |
|---|---|
| 2 tablespoons *Jif* creamy peanut butter | 1 cup milk |
| 2 tablespoons chocolate syrup | 1 scoop chocolate ice cream |

Put all ingredients in a blender and whirl until all ingredients are thoroughly blended.

*Makes 1 serving*

## VANILLA PEANUT BUTTER MILK SHAKE

| | |
|---|---|
| 1 cup ice-cold water | 3 tablespoons *Jif* creamy peanut butter |
| ⅓ cup non-fat dry milk | ½ teaspoon vanilla |

Pour water into blender container. Add the dry milk, JIF peanut butter and vanilla. Cover container and blend until well mixed and frothy. Pour into chilled glass.

*Makes 1 serving*

# PEANUT CHOCOLATE PUNCH

2 cups instant chocolate drink mix
1 quart cold milk
½ cup *Jif* creamy peanut butter
1 tablespoon vanilla
1 quart club soda, chilled
1 quart vanilla ice cream

In a very large bowl, mix the chocolate drink mix, milk, JIF peanut butter and vanilla with a whisk or rotary egg beater until well blended. Stir in the club soda. Pour mixture into tall glasses and top with scoops of vanilla ice cream. Serve at once.

*Makes 12 servings*

# Famous Favorites

## MINNIE PEARL'S GRINDER SWITCH TREATS

½ cup butter
½ cup firmly packed brown sugar
½ cup granulated sugar
1 egg
1 cup *Jif* creamy peanut butter
½ teaspoon salt
½ teaspoon baking soda
1½ cups all-purpose flour, sifted
1 teaspoon vanilla

Beat the butter until soft. Gradually add the sugars. Blend until light and creamy. Beat in the egg, JIF peanut butter, salt and baking soda. Add the flour and vanilla to batter. Mix well. Pinch off pieces of dough and roll them into small balls. Place on a greased baking sheet. Flatten cookies with a fork. Bake in a preheated moderate oven (375° F.) for about 15 minutes.

*Makes about 5 dozen*

# DOROTHY RITTER'S DOUGHNUTS

**DOUGHNUTS**
1 egg, beaten
½ cup milk
½ cup sugar
1 tablespoon peanut oil
1¾ cups all-purpose flour
2 teaspoons baking powder
¼ teaspoon cinnamon
½ teaspoon salt
Peanut oil for frying

**PEANUT BUTTER GLAZE**
½ cup Jif creamy peanut butter
2 cups sifted confectioners' sugar
½ cup milk, about
Chopped peanuts

In a large bowl, blend the egg, milk, sugar, and 1 tablespoon of peanut oil. Sift the dry ingredients together and add to the egg mixture. Dough should be moist. Chill for 1 hour. Put one-third of the mixture on a floured board or floured pastry cloth. Turn over. Roll out to a ⅓-inch thickness. Cut with floured doughnut cutter. Repeat with remaining dough. Gather trimmings together and re-roll, but avoid using additional flour and handle as lightly as possible. Doughnuts should rest on the board after cutting for 10 minutes. Fry doughnuts in 2 inches of peanut oil, preheated to 375° F., until brown (about 2 minutes). Turn with slotted pancake turner and brown the other sides about 1 minute longer. Drain on paper towels. Cool. For glaze, cut the JIF peanut butter into the confectioners' sugar. Slowly blend in enough milk to make soft enough for spreading consistency. Beat until mixture is shiny. Spread on cooled doughnuts. Dip glazed doughnuts into chopped peanuts.

*Makes 18*

# BOBBY BRENNER'S VEAL CUTLETS WITH SPICY PEANUT BUTTER SAUCE

6 large boneless veal cutlets
Salt and pepper
1 egg, well beaten
2 cups rye wafer crumbs
⅓ cup peanut oil

**SAUCE**
2 tablespoons peanut oil
1 small onion, finely chopped
½ green pepper, finely chopped
2 cups tomato puree
½ cup water
½ teaspoon crumbled oregano
1 teaspoon sugar
½ cup *Jif* creamy peanut butter

Pound the veal until very thin. Sprinkle the cutlets on both sides with salt and pepper. Dip cutlets into egg. Coat with crumbs. Press crumbs firmly against the veal. Brown veal on both sides in hot oil, about 4 to 5 minutes on each side. To prepare the sauce, heat the peanut oil and sauté the onion and green pepper until tender. Stir in the tomato puree, water, oregano and sugar. Add the JIF peanut butter and simmer, stirring occasionally, until thick and smooth. Season to taste with salt and pepper. Spoon hot sauce over cutlets.

*Makes 6 servings*

## ANN FLOOD'S CINNAMON ROLLS

**ROLLS**
¾ cup milk
2 tablespoons margarine
⅓ cup mashed potatoes
½ teaspoon salt
3 tablespoons sugar
½ cup *Jif* creamy peanut butter
1 envelope active dry yeast
¼ cup warm (not hot) water
1 egg
3 cups sifted all-purpose flour (about)
Melted butter

**FILLING**
¼ cup softened margarine
⅔ cup sugar
½ teaspoon cinnamon

Scald the milk. Add the margarine, potatoes, salt, sugar and JIF peanut butter, mixing to blend. Cool. Dissolve the yeast in the ¼ cup of warm water. Add yeast and egg to milk mixture. Add 1 cup of flour and beat about 1 minute. Gradually add as much more flour as can be easily beaten into the dough (about 1½ cups). Knead dough on a lightly floured board until smooth and satiny, using additional flour as needed. Place in a greased bowl, brush top with melted butter. Let rise in a warm place until double in bulk. Roll dough on a lightly floured board to a 9 × 16-inch rectangle, ¼ inch thick. To make filling, cream the margarine, sugar and cinnamon. Spread on dough. Roll up as for a jelly roll, beginning at the 16-inch side. Cut into 1-inch slices. Place cut side up close together in a greased 9-inch-square pan. Brush tops with melted butter. Cover and let rise in a warm place until double in bulk. Bake in a hot oven (400° F.) for about 20 to 25 minutes, or until crusty and browned.

Makes 16

## IRVING WAUGH'S PEANUT BUTTER STUFFED PORK ROAST

¼ cup butter or margarine
1 large onion, chopped
2 apples, peeled, cored and chopped
½ cup raisins
⅓ cup Jif creamy peanut butter
1 package (7 ounces) toasted croutons

1 pork roast (4 pounds)
Salt and pepper

**SAUCE**
1 jar (15½ ounces) spaghetti sauce
2 tablespoons Jif creamy peanut butter

In a skillet, heat the butter and sauté the onion until golden. Add the chopped apples. Stir for another 5 minutes. Add the raisins and ⅓ cup of JIF peanut butter. Stir until the peanut butter is melted and the mixture is well blended. Stir in the croutons. Rub roast with salt and pepper. With a sharp knife, cut along the ribs of the pork roast, down toward the bottom of the roast, starting and ending 1 inch from edges of meat. This will form a large pocket. Stuff pocket with some of the stuffing. Spoon the remaining stuffing into a small greased 3-cup casserole. Cover and aside. Cover meat with foil and roast in a preheated moderate oven (350° F.) for 2 hours. Place casserole of stuffing in the oven for 30 minutes before roast is done. In a saucepan, mix the spaghetti sauce and JIF peanut butter. Heat until bubbly. Slice pork roast and spoon sauce over meat.

*Makes 6 servings*

# BILL ANDERSON'S HAM LOAF

**LOAF**
2 pounds ground smoked ham
¾ cup fine dry breadcrumbs
2 large eggs
¾ cup milk
¼ cup *Jif* creamy peanut butter
⅓ cup chopped onion
1 teaspoon dry mustard
4 slices bacon

**SAUCE**
1¼ cups (10¼ ounces) beef gravy
1 cup catsup
¼ cup *Jif* creamy peanut butter
1 tablespoon minced onion
Water

Combine all loaf ingredients except the bacon. Press mixture into a greased 9 × 5 × 3-inch loaf pan. Cover the top with the bacon slices. Bake in a preheated moderate oven (350° F.) for 1 hour or until firm. Cool in pan for 5 minutes. Loosen edges with a knife and invert on a platter. Combine all sauce ingredients except water and simmer until bubbly. Gradually blend in enough water to make sauce the right consistency. Spoon sauce over slices of ham loaf.

*Makes 6 servings*

## HARPER EDWARDS' SKILLET PEANUT HASH

¼ cup butter or margarine
1 large onion, chopped
1 green pepper, chopped
⅓ cup Jif creamy peanut butter
½ cup catsup
1 cup (1 pint) light cream
4 large potatoes, cooked, peeled and diced
3 cups diced, cooked leftover beef, chicken or turkey
Salt and pepper
Green pepper rings

Sauté the onion and chopped green pepper in the butter until golden, about 5 minutes. Stir in the JIF peanut butter, catsup and cream. When mixture begins to bubble, stir in the potatoes and meat. Stir to blend well. Season to taste with salt and pepper. Serve hot garnished with green pepper rings.
*Makes 6 servings*

## HERBERT GRANATH'S APPLE RAISIN FRITTERS

2 eggs
½ cup milk
¼ cup sugar
1½ cups all-purpose flour
1 teaspoon baking powder
1 teaspoon salt
1 teaspoon peanut oil
4 medium-sized cooking apples, peeled, cored and diced
½ cup raisins
1 teaspoon nutmeg or cinnamon
Deep peanut oil, heated to 375°
1 cup granulated sugar mixed with grated rind of 1 lemon

In a bowl, beat the eggs and stir in the milk, sugar, flour, baking powder, salt and oil. Fold in the apples, raisins and spice. Drop by heaping tablespoons into hot peanut oil. Fry 3 to 4 minutes or until brown on all sides. Drain on absorbent paper. Roll warm fritters in the sugar mixture and serve warm, or serve with maple syrup and sausage or bacon. Delicious with scrambled eggs for brunch.

*Makes 6 servings*

## MY MOTHER'S PEANUT BUTTER FRUIT CRISP

- 1 teaspoon pumpkin pie spice
- 1 can (1 pound, 4 ounces) pineapple chunks, undrained
- 1 can (1 pound, 4 ounces) pie-sliced apples, drained
- 1 can (1 pound, 4 ounces) sliced peaches, drained
- 1 can (1 pound, 4 ounces) pear halves, drained
- ⅓ cup chopped dried apricots
- ¼ cup *Jif* creamy peanut butter
- ¼ cup firmly packed brown sugar
- ¼ cup butter or margarine
- 2 cups granola

In a large bowl, mix the spice and fruits. Divide the mixture equally between three 9 × 2-inch round casseroles. In another bowl, combine the remaining ingredients, mixing until soft and crumbly. Sprinkle crumbly mixture evenly over fruit. Bake one casserole in a moderate oven (350° F.) for 30 minutes or until brown. Cover the other two casseroles closely with foil and freeze until hard. When you wish to make them part of your menu, bake from frozen state in a moderate oven

(350° F.) for 45 minutes, keeping casserole covered for the first 20 minutes of cooking.

*Makes 8-serving casserole*

## FOUR SEASONS PEANUT BOURBON LAYER CAKE

**CAKE**
1 cup fine ground, not powdered, peanuts
5 large eggs
2 egg yolks
7 ounces (1 cup minus 2 tablespoons) granulated sugar
3½ ounces (½ cup minus 1 tablespoon) cake flour
3½ ounces cornstarch
1½ tablespoons bourbon

**BOURBON SYRUP**
½ cup granulated sugar
¼ cup water
2 tablespoons bourbon

**PEANUT BUTTER CREAM**
3 egg whites
3 tablespoons water
3 ounces (¼ cup plus 2 tablespoons) granulated sugar
12 ounces (3 sticks) unsalted butter, softened
¼ cup confectioners' sugar
3 ounces (¼ cup plus 2 tablespoons) *Jif* creamy peanut butter
3 tablespoons bourbon
Confectioners' sugar for decoration

Preheat the oven to 375° F. Butter a 9 × 2-inch round layer-cake pan and line it with half of the ground peanuts. Set aside. In a large mixing bowl, combine the eggs, egg yolks and the 7 ounces of sugar and stir together over very low heat (or hot water) for 2 minutes. Remove from heat. Beat for about 12 minutes or until the mixture becomes very thick and pale. (A dollop suspended from the end of a finger should not budge.) Combine the flour, cornstarch and remaining ground peanuts. Fold bourbon into the beaten egg mixture, then gently fold in flour mixture, a little at a time, being careful not to deflate batter. Turn batter into cake pan and bake for 35 minutes or until cake is springy to the touch and has shrunk slightly from the sides of the pan. Cool for 10 to 15 minutes before unmolding. The cake must be thoroughly cooled before slicing and filling.

Make the bourbon syrup while the cake is baking and cooling, as it must also be completely cooled before using. In a small saucepan, place the ½ cup sugar and ¼ cup water. Simmer gently for several minutes or until sugar is completely dissolved. Remove from heat. When syrup has cooled, stir in the 2 tablespoons of bourbon.

To prepare the butter cream filling, place the egg whites in a mixing bowl and beat with an electric mixer (not a hand mixer) until soft peaks form. Prepare syrup by combining 3 tablespoons of water and 3 ounces of sugar in a small saucepan. Bring to a boil and continue boiling until syrup reaches 235° F. on a candy thermometer (the soft-ball stage). As the syrup comes to a boil, swirl the liquid several times in the pan to be sure sugar is completely dissolved. With the mixer running, pour syrup in a thin stream onto the beaten egg whites (this produces a meringue). Continue beating at medium speed or until the meringue is completely cool (about 10 minutes). Meanwhile, beat the butter until soft and fluffy. Add butter by teaspoonfuls to the cooled meringue, always with the mixer running. Beat until very smooth, beating in an extra ¼ cup of confectioners' sugar if the mixture does not become smooth and homogeneous. Once it has become smooth and creamy, add the JIF peanut butter and 3 tablespoons of bourbon. Beat until thoroughly blended.

Slice the cake horizontally into three layers of equal thickness. Set aside the top layer which is not coated with ground peanuts. Place the middle layer on a plate and spoon half of the bourbon syrup over the cut surface. Spread half the peanut butter cream evenly over this and place the last layer on top, peanut-coated side up. Spread the remaining butter cream over the top and sides of the cake. Break the reserved cake layer into pieces and rub rapidly between the hands to make crumbs. Spread the crumbs over the top and sides of the cake and press them into place with a spatula. Place a decorative stencil or paper doily on top of cake and sprinkle with confectioners' sugar.

*Note:* all ingredient quantities given in ounces are volume ounces rather than weight ounces, except the 12 ounces of butter used in the butter cream.

# Index

A-1 Sauce, 81
Acorn squash, peanut filled, 69-70
African Chicken with Groundnut Sauce, 40
African Sweet Potatoes and Bananas, 65
Alabama Prize Peanut Butter Cake, 134-35
All-Homemade Peanut Butter Squares, The, 107
Almond extract in candy, 159
Amino acids in peanut butter, 14
Ann Flood's Cinnamon Rolls, 169
Appetizers, 19-27
    Crunchy Peanut Olives, 21-22
    Diablo Peanut Dip, 25
    Hot Bacon, Ham and Peanut Roll-ups, 27
    Maho Bay Camp Mushrooms, 27
    Maho Bay Camp Pâté, 19
    Pat Gack's Meatballs, 20
    Peanut and Ham Stuffed Mushrooms, 21
    Peanut and Onion Canapés, 20
    Peanut Butter Bacon Canapés, 23
    Peanut Butter Cheese Dip, 24
    Peanut Butter Chicken Dip, 24-25
    Peanut Butter Dip, 22
    Peanut Cheese Rolls, 26
    Peanut Chops, 26
    Peanut Pineapple Dip, 22
    Peanut Sticks, 25
Apple Crumble, 130
Apples
    in cakes, 129-30
    in cookies, 101-02
    dumplings, 145-46
    in fluff, 142-43
    in fruit crisp, 173-74
    in muffins, 96-97
    with pork chops, 51, 54
    with pork roast, 170
    raisin fritters, 172-73
Apricot Peanut Butter Drops, 157
Apricots
    in candy, 157, 158
    in fruit crisp, 173-74
Autumn Festival Crisp, 142-43

# 178 INDEX

B vitamins in peanut butter, 12, 14
Bacon
  breads, 90, 91
  canapés, 23
  corn muffins, 97
  in ham loaf, 171
  in protein burgers, 46-47
  in rollups, 27
Baked Ham Rolls Georgia, 52-53
Baked Spaghetti Augusta, 62
Baked Stuffed Tomatoes, 74
Bama Peanut-Banana Bread with Orange Glaze, 94
Bananas
  Bama Peanut-Banana Bread with Orange Glaze, 94
  beverage, 162-63
  cake, 137
  with chicken, 40
  cookies, 110-11
  and sweet potatoes, 65
Barbecue Sauce Savannah, 82
Battlefield Fufu, 39-40
Beans
  green, in vegetable platter, 71
  *See also* Lentils
Beef
  broth, in Sudanese Shorba, 31
  chuck
    Birmingham, 43
    meat loaf, 47
    peanut turnovers, 46
    spicy roast, 45
  leftover, in hash, 172
  meatballs, 20
  stews, 44-45
  *See also* Veal
Beef Birmingham, 43
Beverages, 162-65
  Chocolate Peanut Butter Milk Shake, 164
  Good Health Breakfast in a Glass, 162-63
  Hot Maple Peanut Drink, 163
  Orange Peanut Nog, 162
  Peanut Butter Maple Milk Shake, 164
  Peanut Chocolate Punch, 165
  Vanilla Peanut Butter Milk Shake 164
Bill Anderson's Ham Loaf, 171
Bobby Brenner's Veal Cutlets with Spicy Peanut Butter Sauce, 168
Bourbon Syrup, 174-76
Braised Celery with Peanut-Soy Sauce, 73
Breads, 88-98
  bacon, 91
  bacon onion, 90
  Bama peanut-banana, with orange glaze, 94
  basic peanut butter, 88-89
  glazed raisin, 93
  muffins, *see* Muffins
  orange knots, 89
  Peanut Butter Fruit Baskets, 98
  pinwheel, 92-93
  raisin braid, 89
  rye, Peanut Chops from, 26
  Tangy Fruitbread, 95
  *See also* Rolls
Breakfast beverage, 162-63
Brown betty, 139
Brownies, marbled, 113
Bride's Fingers, 108
Brussels Sprouts with Peanuts, 72-73

Cakes, 124-38
  Alabama Prize Peanut Butter, 134-35
  Apple Crumble, 130
  Atlanta Apple Peanut, 129-30
  Double Fudge Peanut Butter, 132

# INDEX

Four Seasons Peanut Bourbon Layer Cake, 174-76
Georgia Prize Peanut Refrigerator Cake, 150
Meringue Shells with Chocolate Peanut Filling, 131
Party Layer Cake, 137-38
Peanut Brittle Cheesecake, 128
Peanut Butter Cake, 138
Peanut Butter Carrot Delight, 136
Peanut Butter Chocolate Roll, 127-28
Peanut Butter Coconut Cake, 135
Peanut Butter Ice-Cream, 149
Peanut Butter Molasses Squares, 129
Peanut Butter Picnic Cake, 125
Peanut Butter Roll with Cranberry Filling, 133-34
Peanut-flavored Vacherin, 126-27
Peanut Orange Cake, 124
Peanutty Banana Cake, 137
Spice Cupcakes, 125-26
Canapés, *see* Appetizers
Candy, 151-61
Apricot Peanut Butter Drops, 157
Chocolate Peanut Logs, 156-57
Christmas Peanut Butter Moons, 156
Easy Chocolate Peanut Butter Fudge, 160
Fig Peanut Fudge, 151
Grand Prize Peanut Butter Candy, 161
Orange Peanut Divinity, 158
Peanut Butter Dateballs, 152
Peanut Butter Fudge, 153
Peanut Butter Oats Supreme, 159
Peanut Butter Panocha, 153-54
Peanut Butter Pralines, 154
Peanut Butter Prune Roll, 152
Peanut Fruit Balls, 158
Peanut Health Candy, 154-55
Peanut-Raisin Balls, 159
Vanilla Peanut Divinity, 155
Cantaloupe in fruit salad, 77-78
Carrots
beef ragout, 44-45
cake, 136
and celery, peanut-sauced, 72
in chicken pie, 34-35
with squash, 70
with veal, 50
in vegetable platter, 71
Carver, George Washington, 10
Casseroles
fruit crisp, 173-74
sweet potato-peanut butter, 65-66
Cauliflower with Spicy Peanut Butter Sauce, 71-72
Celery
braised, with peanut-soy sauce, 73
carrots and, 72
Chattahoochee Crunchies, 110
Cheese
American
in Baked Spaghetti Augusta, 62
in hot peanut and onion canapés, 20
in sauce, 85-86

# INDEX

Cheese (*cont.*)
  Cheddar
    in cheese dip, 24
    in peanut and ham stuffed mushrooms, 21
    in peanut stuffed peppers, 63
    in peanut vegetable loaf, 61-62
    in potatoes au gratin, 67-68
    in protein burgers, 46-47
    in sauce, 85-86
  cream
    in cheesecake, 128
    in fluff, 142-43
    in fruit dressing, 79
    with peanut butter, olives, 21-22
    salad, with peanut butter and tomatoes, 75
  Muenster, in Peruvian Potatoes Supreme, 68
  Old English spread, in peanut rolls, 26
  Swiss, in sauce, 85-86
Cheesecake, peanut brittle, 128
Chicken
  African, with groundnut sauce, 40
  in Battlefield Fufu, 39-40
  chop, 48
  cutlets, with spicy peanut butter sauce, 37-38
  dip, 24-25
  individual stuffed halves, 35-36
  Indonesian, with paprika, 42-43
  leftover, in hash, 172
  liver
    Maho Bay Camp pâté, 19
    spicy, 41
  one-dish meal with peanuts, 32-33
  and seafood, Indonesia, 60
  with spiced fruit peanut stuffing, 54-55
  stock or broth, in soup, 28
Chicken and Seafood Indonesia, 60
Chicken Djakarta, 38-39
Chicken in Honey Peanut Butter Sauce, 39
Chicken Moamba, 37
Chicken Pie with Sweet Potato-Peanut Crust, 34-35
Chicken Punjab, 33-34
Chicken with Peanut Sauce, 36-37
Chili peppers
  in sauce, 85-86
  in stew, 41-42
Chili sauce, 71, 80
Chocolate
  in cakes, 125, 126-27, 132
  in candy, 156-57, 160
  in cookies, 111-13, 122
  in ice-box torte frosting, 147
  in peanut cream cones, 148
  in pie, 144
  punch, 165
  *See also* Cocoa
Chocolate Peanut Butter Milk Shake, 164
Chocolate Peanut Butter Thins, 121
Chocolate Peanut Logs, 156-57
Chocolate roll, 127-28
Chocolate sandwich cookies, 115-16
Chow mein noodles in cookies, 123
Christmas Peanut Butter Moons, 156
"Chunky" peanut butter, 16
Cinnamon
  in beverage, 163
  in bread, 93, 96-97, 98
  in brown betty, 139
  in cakes, 124-26, 129-30
  in candy, 152
  in chicken dishes, 36-37

# INDEX

in cookies, 101, 104, 108, 110-11, 117, 119
in doughnuts, 167
in fluff, 142-43
in fritters, 172-73
in ice cream balls, 146
rolls, 169
in soup, 31
Cocoa
in candy, 159
in cookies, 106, 110, 120, 121
in refrigerator cake, 150
*See also* Chocolate
Coconut
cake, 135
in candy, 152, 156-57, 159
in cookies, 102, 110, 112-13
with groundnut chop, 48
Coconut-Peanut Sauce for Kebobs, 86-87
Coconut Water, 86-87
Cod fillets, Okefenokee, 58-59
Coffee
in cookies, 120
in frozen mousse, 146-47
in refrigerator cake, 150
Cold Peanut Butter Vegetable Potage, 29
Cookies, 99-123
Bride's Fingers, 108
Chattahoochee Crunchies, 110
Chinese Chocolate Peanut Clusters, 123
Chocolate Peanut Butter Thins, 121
Crunchy Peanut Cookies, 114-15
Honey Peanut Ice-box Slices, 119
Italian Peanut Cookies, 106
Kenley's Cinnamon Crinkles, 104-05
Maho Bay Mounds, 112-13
Marbled Peanut Butter Brownies, 113
Minnie Pearl's Grinder Switch Treats, 166
Nut Butter Crescents, 120-21
Oatmeal Refrigerator Cookies, 109
Orange Peanut Rummies, 108-09
Peanut-Apple Teardrops, 101-02
Peanut-Banana Oatmeal Specials, 110-11
Peanut Bars, 104
Peanut Brittle Kisses, 118-19
Peanut Butter Crisps, 114
Peanut Butter Daisy Cups, 105
Peanut Butter-Date Refrigerator Cookies, 117
Peanut Butter Horseshoes, 120
Peanut Butter Lemon Ice Box Cookies, 118
Peanut Butter Wheat Drops, 99
Peanut Chocolate Chip Cookies, 122
Peanut Chocolate Sandwich Cookies, 115-16
Peanut-Date Meringue Balls, 116
Peanut Health Munchies, 101-02
Peanut Marshmallow Squares, 112
Persian Peanut Drops, 102
Protein Peanut Butter Breakfast Cookies, 103
Scottish Peanut Butter Scones with Lemon Curd, 100
Superior Peanut Butter Cookies, 111
The All-Homemade Peanut Butter Squares, 107
Corn in ham fritters, 52

Cornflakes
in chicken cutlets, 37-38
in cookies, 114-15
in hush puppies and trout, 57
in peanut chops, 26
Cornmeal, 57
in bread, 88-89
Corn muffins, peanut-bacon, 97
Corn syrup
in baked ham rolls, 52-53
in candy, 151, 155, 158
Crabmeat in Chicken and Seafood Indonesia, 60
Cranberry Filling, 133-34
Cream of Peanut Soup, 28
Creamy Peanut Butter Mold, 140
Creamy Peanut Tomato Soup, 30
Crunchy Peanut Cookies, 114-15
Crunchy Peanut Olives, 21-22
Cupcakes, spices, 125-26

Dates
in candy, 152, 158
in cookies, 102, 117
Desserts, 139-50
Autumn Festival Fluff, 142-43
Chilled Peanut Butter Soufflé, 141
Creamy Peanut Butter Mold, 140
Frozen Peanut Brittle Mousse, 146-47
Frozen Peanut Butter Pie, 141-42
Frozen Peanut Mousse Pie, 144
Peanut Butter Apple Dumplings with Lemon Sauce, 145-46
Peanut Butter Ice-Box Torte, 147
Peanut Cream Cones, 148
Sour Cream Chiffon Pie, 143
*See also* Cakes; Cookies
Diablo Peanut Dip, 25
Dips
chicken, 24-25
diablo, 25
pineapple, 22
sour cream, 22
Dixie Potato Salad, 77
Dorothy Ritter's Doughnuts, 167
Double Fudge Peanut Butter Cake, 132
Doughnuts, 167

Easy Chocolate Peanut Butter Fudge, 160
Eggs
hard-cooked, 41-42, 68, 71, 78, 80
in one-dish meal, 32-33
in peanut stuffed peppers, 63
in protein burgers, 47

Fig Peanut Fudge, 151
Fillings
for apple dumplings, 145-46
chocolate-peanut, for meringues, 131
for chocolate sandwich cookies, 115-16
for cinnamon rolls, 169
cranberry, 133-34
for frozen mousse pie, 144
peanut butter cream, 174-76
for vacherin, 126-27
Fish
Okefenokee Fish Fillets, 58-59
Peanut Butter Hush Puppies with Fried Trout, 57
Peanut Country Fish Fry, 59-60
Florunner peanuts, 11
Flounder in fish fry, 59-60

# INDEX

Fluff
  autumn festival, 142-43
  in fudge, 160
  marshmallow fruit salad, 81
Four Seasons Peanut Bourbon Layer Cake, 174-76
Fritters
  apple raisin, 172-73
  ham, 52
Frosting
  for cakes, 133-35, 136
  for ice-box torte, 147
  orange rum, 106
  *See also* Topping
Frozen cookies, *see* Refrigerator cookies
Frozen Peanut Brittle Mousse, 146-47
Frozen peanut cream cones, 148
Frozen Peanut Mousse Pie, 144
Fruit balls, 158
Fruit baskets, 98
Fruit crisp, 173-74
Fruit Salad with Peanut Butter-Pineapple Dressing, 77-78
Fruit salads, *see* Salads—fruit
Fruitbread, 95
Fudge, 153
  easy, 160
  fig peanut, 151
Fudge cake, 132

Georgia Prize Peanut Refrigerator Cake, 150
Ghanian Stew, 44
Glazed Peanut Butter Raisin Loaf, 93
Gone With the Wind Fritters, 52
Good Health Breakfast in a Glass, 162-63
Graham crackers
  in candy, 152, 156-57, 161
  in cookies, 112-13
  in fluff, 142-43
  in ice cream balls, 146
  in pies, 141-42, 144
Grand Prize Peanut Butter Candy, 161
Granola in fruit crisp, 173-74
Grapefruit in salad dressing, 79
Grapes in fruit salad, 77-78
Green peppers
  in cheese dip, 24
  in hash, 172
  lentil and peanut stuffed, 64
  in main dishes, 32-34
  peanut stuffed, 63
  in Spinach Afrique, 69
Groundnut Chop, 48
Groundnut Sauce, 40
Groundnut Stew, 41-42

Haddock fillets, Okefenokee, 58-59
Ham
  in Chicken and Seafood Indonesia, 60
  deviled, in dip, 25
  in roll-ups, 27
  in stuffed mushrooms, 21
  fritters, 52
  loaf, 171
  puffs, 23
  rolls, 52-53
Harper Edwards' Skillet Peanut Hash, 172
Hash, skillet, 172
Herbert Granath's Apple Raisin Fritters, 172-73
Honey
  in beverage, 162-63
  in candy, 154-55, 157
  in cookies, 108, 119
  in frozen mousse, 146-47
  in fruit dressings, 79, 80
  in topping for cookies, 107
Honey Peanut Butter Sauce, 39
Honey Peanut Ice-Box Slices, 119
Horseradish, 46, 86

# INDEX

Horseshoes, peanut butter, 120
Hot Bacon, Ham and Peanut Roll-ups, 27
Hot Maple Peanut Drink, 163
Hot Peanut and Onion Canapés, 20
Hush puppies, peanut butter, 57

Ice-box cookies, *see* Refrigerator cookies
Ice-box torte, 147
Ice cream balls, 146
Ice cream cake, 149
Individual Stuffed Chicken Halves, 35-36
Indonesian dishes
    Chicken and Seafood Indonesia, 60
    Chicken Djakarta, 38-39
    chicken with paprika, 43
    lamb kebobs, 42
    vegetable platter, 71
Indonesian Chicken, 43
Indonesian Lamb Kebobs, 42
Indonesian Vegetable Platter, 71
Irving Waugh's Peanut Butter Stuffed Pork Roast, 170

Juniper berries, 84-85

Kebobs
    coconut-peanut sauce for, 86-87
    lamb, Indonesian, 42
Kenley's Cinnamon Crinkles, 104-05
Kisses, peanut brittle, 118-19

Lamb
    chop, 48
    kebobs, Indonesian, 42
    stew, 41-42
Layered Peanut-Orange Salad, 76
Leftovers in hash, 172

Lemon Curd, 100
Lemon ice box cookies, 118
Lemon rind
    in cake, 130
    in cookies, 118
    in fritters, 172-73
Lemon Sauce, 145-46
Lentil-Peanut Stuffed Peppers, 64
Lentils
    burgers, 61
    stuffed peppers, 64

Maho Bay Camp Mushrooms, 27
Maho Bay Camp Pâté, 19
Maho Bay Mounds, 112-13
Main dishes, 32-62
    African Chicken, 40
    Baked Ham Rolls Georgia, 52-53
    Baked Spaghetti Augusta, 62
    Battlefield Fufu, 39-40
    Beef Birmingham, 43
    Bill Anderson's Ham Loaf, 171
    Bobby Brenner's Veal Cutlets with Spicy Peanut Butter Sauce, 168
    Chicken and Seafood Indonesia, 60
    Chicken Cutlets with Spicy Peanut Butter Sauce, 37-38
    Chicken Djakarta, 38-39
    Chicken in Honey Peanut Butter Sauce, 39
    Chicken Moamba, 37
    Chicken-Peanut One-Dish Meal, 32-33
    Chicken Pie with Sweet Potato-Peanut Crust, 34-35
    Chicken Punjab, 33-34
    Chicken with Peanut Sauce, 36-37

# INDEX

Gone With the Wind Fritters, 52
Ghanian Stew, 44
Groundnut Chop, 48
Groundnut Stew, 41-42
Harper Edwards' Skillet Peanut Hash, 172
Individual Stuffed Chicken Halves, 35-36
Indonesian Chicken, 43
Indonesian Lamb Kebobs, 42
Irving Waugh's Peanut Butter Stuffed Pork Roast, 170
Okefenokee Fish Fillets, 58-59
Peanut Butter-Beef Loaf, 47
Peanut Butter Hush Puppies with Fried Trout, 57
Peanut Butter Lentil Burgers, 61
Peanut Butter Pork Chop and Sweet Potato Casserole, 55
Peanut Butter Protein Burgers, 46-47
Peanut Butter Stuffed Pork Chops, 51
Peanut Country Fish Fry, 59-60
Peanut Meat Turnovers, 46
Peanut Vegetable Loaf, 61-62
Peruvian Veal in Peanut Sauce, 50
Pork Chops (or Chicken) with Spiced Fruit Peanut Stuffings, 55
Pork Roast with Brazilian Peanut Sauce, 53
Roast Veal with Peanut Butter Sauce, 48-49
Shrimp Tahiti, 58
Southern Ragout, 44-45
Spicy Chicken Livers Southeast, 41
Spicy Chuck Roast, 45
Spicy Pork Sate, 56
Veal Chops with Spicy Peanut Butter Sauce, 49

Maple drinks, 163-64
Marbled Peanut Butter Brownies, 113
Marshmallow fluff
  in fudge, 160
  peanut butter fruit salad, 81
Marshmallow squares, 112
Mayonnaise, strawberry-peanut, 78
Meat loaf, peanut butter-beef, 47
Meatballs, Pat Gack's, 20
Meringue balls, peanut-date, 116
Meringue Shells with Chocolate Peanut Filling, 131
Milk shakes, *see* Beverages
Minnie Pearl's Grinder Switch Treats, 166
Molasses bread, 88-89
Molasses squares, 129
Mold, creamy, 140
Mounds, 112-13
Mousse, frozen
  peanut brittle, 146-47
  pie, 144
Muffins
  peanut-bacon corn, 97
  peanut butter apple, 96-97
Mushrooms
  Maho Bay Camp, 27
  in one-dish meal, 32-33
  peanut and ham stuffed, 21
My Mother's Peanut Butter Fruit Crisp, 173-74

Nut Butter Crescents, 120-21

Oatmeal
  in candy, 159
  in cookies, 108-10
  in marshmallow squares, 112

# INDEX

Oatmeal Refrigerator Cookies, 109
Okefenokee Fish Fillets, 58-59
Olives
  in cheese rolls, 26
  crunchy peanuts, 21-22
  in Peruvian Potatoes, 68
Onions
  in bread, 90
  canapés, 20
  in sauces, 83, 85-86
  in soups, 29
  in vegetable dishes, 63-64, 66, 69-70, 73, 74
Orange gelatin in Creamy Peanut Butter Mold, 140
Orange glaze, Bama peanut-banana Bread with, 94
Orange Knots Peanut Butter Bread, 89
Orange juice
  in baked ham rolls, 52-53
  in bread, 92-93
  in cake, 124, 135, 136
  in nog, 162
  in pork chops, 54
Orange Peanut Divinity, 158
Orange Peanut Nog, 162
Orange Peanut Rummies, 108-09
Orange rind
  in baked ham rolls, 52-53
  in bread, 92-93, 94, 95
  in cake, 128, 131, 132, 135, 136
  in chilled soufflé, 141
  in pork chop, 55
  in salad, 76
  with sweet potatoes and bananas, 65
Orange Rum Frosting, 106
Oranges
  with chicken, 40
  in layered salad, 76
  with Spicy Pork Sate, 56
  in sweet potato casserole, 65-66

Panocha, 153-54
Party Layer Cake, 137-38
Pat Gack's Meatballs, 20
Pâté, Maho Bay Camp, 19
Peaches
  in fruit crisp, 173-74
  in fruit salad, 77-78
  Peanut and Ham Stuffed Mushrooms, 21
Peanut-Banana Oatmeal Specials, 110-11
Peanut Bars, 104
Peanut Brittle Cheesecake, 128
Peanut Brittle Kisses, 118-19
Peanut brittle mousse, 146-47
Peanut butter, 11-14
  FDA requirements for, 13
  methods of making, 14-16
  nutritive value of, 12-14
Peanut Butter Apple Dumplings with Lemon Sauce, 145-46
Peanut Butter Apple Muffins, 96-97
Peanut Butter Bacon Bread, 91
Peanut Butter Bacon Canapés, 23
Peanut Butter Bacon Onion Bread, 90
Peanut Butter-Beef Meat Loaf, 47
Peanut Butter Bread, 88-89
Peanut Butter Brown Betty, 139
Peanut Butter Cake, 138
Peanut Butter Carrot Delight, 136
Peanut Butter Chantilly Sauce, 86
Peanut Butter Chicken Dip, 24-25
Peanut Butter Chocolate Roll, 127-28
Peanut Butter Coconut Cake, 135
Peanut Butter Cream, 174-76

# INDEX

Peanut Butter-Cream Cheese Tomato Salad, 75
Peanut Butter Crisps, 114
Peanut Butter Daisy Cups, 105
Peanut Butter-Date Refrigerator Cookies, 117
Peanut Butter Dateballs, 152
Peanut Butter Dip, 22
Peanut Butter Fruit Baskets, 98
Peanut Butter Fudge, 153
Peanut Butter Ham Puffs, 23
Peanut Butter Horseshoes, 102
Peanut Butter Hush Puppies with Fried Trout, 57
Peanut Butter Ice-Box Torte, 147
Peanut Butter Ice Cream Balls, 146
Peanut Butter Ice Cream Cake, 149
Peanut Butter Lentil Burgers, 61
Peanut Butter Maple Milk Shake, 163-64
Peanut Butter Molasses Squares, 129
Peanut Butter Oats Supreme, 159
Peanut Butter Panocha, 153-54
Peanut Butter Picnic Cake, 125
Peanut Butter Pinwheel Loaf, 92-93
Peanut Butter Pork Chops and Sweet Potato Casserole, 55
Peanut Butter Pralines, 154
Peanut Butter Protein Burgers, 46-47
Peanut Butter Prune Roll, 152
Peanut Butter Roll with Cranberry Filling, 133-34
Peanut butter sauce
 for barbecue, 82, 83
 carrots and celery with, 72
 cauliflower with, spicy, 71-72
 Chantilly sauce, 86
 chicken with, 36-37
  African, 40
  cutlets with spicy sauce, 37-38
  honey sauce, 39
 coconut, for kebobs, 86-87
 for game, 84-85
 hot, 83
 for main dishes, 84
 Peruvian, 85-86
 pork with, 53, 170
 spicy, 37-38, 49, 85, 168
 veal with, 48-50, 168
Peanut Butter Stuffed Pork Chops, 51
Peanut Butter Thousand Isle Dressing, 80
Peanut Butter Wheat Rolls, 96
Peanut Cheese Rolls, 26
Peanut Chocolate Chip Cookies, 122
Peanut Chocolate Punch, 165
Peanut-Chocolate Sandwich Cookies, 115-16
Peanut Chops, 26
Peanut clusters, Chinese chocolate, 123
Peanut Country Fish Fry, 59-60
Peanut Cream Cones, 148
Peanut-Date Meringue Balls, 116
Peanut Filled Acorn Squash, 69-70
Peanut-flavored Vacherin, 126-27
Peanut Fruit Balls, 158
Peanut Health Candy, 154-55
Peanut Health Munchies, 101
Peanut Marshmallow Squares, 112
Peanut Orange Cake, 124
Peanut Pineapple Dip, 22
Peanut Potatoes au Gratin, 67-68

# INDEX

Peanut-Raisin Balls, 159
Peanut-sauced Carrots and
  Celery, 72
Peanut Soup Creole, 29
Peanut Sticks, 25
Peanut Stuffed Peppers, 63
Peanut Surprise Fruit
  Dressing, 79
Peanut Vegetable Loaf, 61-62
Peanuts, history of, 9-12
Peanutty Banana Cake, 137
Peanutty Festival Squash, 70
Pears in fruit crisp, 173-74
Peas
  in peanut vegetable loaf,
    61-62
  with veal, 50
Peppers, chili
  in sauce, 85-86
  in stew, 41-42
Peppers, green
  in cheese dip, 24
  in hash, 172
  lentil-peanut stuffed, 64
  in main dishes, 32-34
  peanut stuffed, 63
  in Spinach Afrique, 69
Peppers, red, 58, 60, 71, 82
Persian Peanut Drops, 102
Peruvian Peanut Sauce, 85-86
Peruvian Potatoes Supreme,
  68
Peruvian Veal in Peanut
  Sauce, 50
Pies
  frozen, 141-42
    peanut mousse, 144
    sour cream chiffon, 143
Pimento, 70
Pineapple
  with chicken, 33-34
  dip, 22
  in fruit crisp, 173-74
  in fruit salad, 77-78
Pineapple juice
  in fruit dressings, 79, 80
  in fruit salad fluff, 81

Plantation Grapefruit Peanut
  Butter Dressing, 79
Pork
  chops
    peanut butter stuffed, 51
    with spiced fruit peanut
      stuffing, 54
    and sweet potato
      casserole, 55
  roast, with Brazilian peanut
    sauce, 53
  peanut butter stuffed, 170
Potatoes
  au gratin, peanut, 67-68
  in hash, 172
  in main dishes, 34-35
  Peruvian, Supreme, 68
  salad, Dixie, 77
  sweet, *see* Sweet potatoes
Pralines, 154
Protein in peanut butter, 11-14
Protein Peanut Butter Breakfast Cookies, 103
Prunes
  in candy, 152, 158
  in fruit basket, 98
Pumpkin, peanutty festival, 70
Punch, chocolate, 165

Quick Peanut Soup, 30

Raisin Braid Peanut Butter
  Bread, 89
Raisins
  in apple dumplings, 145-46
  apple fritters, 172-73
  in bread, 92-93, 95
  in brown betty, 139
  in cake, 136
  in candy, 159
  with chicken, 33-34
  in cookies, 101-03, 112-13,
    114-15
  in pork roast, 170
Refrigerator cake, 150
Refrigerator cookies (ice box
  cookies)
  honey, 119

## INDEX

lemon, 118
oatmeal, 109
Rice
  with beef dishes, 43-45
  brown, in protein burgers, 46-47
  with chicken, 33-34, 36-37, 48
  with chicken and seafood, 60
  with lamb, 41-42, 48
  with shrimp, 58
Roast Veal with Peanut Butter Sauce, 48-49
Rolls
  baked ham, 52-53
  chocolate, 127-28
  cinnamon, 169
  peanut butter wheat, 96
  peanut cheese, 26
Rum cookies, 108-09
Rum in peanut butter dressing, 79

Salad dressings
  fruit
    à la Dothan, 80
    peanut butter-pineapple, 77-78
    peanut surprise, 79
    plantation grapefruit, 79
  grapefruit peanut butter, 79
  peanut, 78
  peanut butter-pineapple, 77-78
  peanut butter thousand isle, 80
  peanut butter vegetable, 81
  peanut fruit, 79
Salads, 75-81
  Dixie Potato Salad, 77
  fruit
    Fruit Salad with Peanut Butter-Pineapple Dressing, 77-78
    Layered Peanut and Orange Salad, 76
    Peanut Butter Fruit Salad Fluff, 81
    Peanut Butter-Cream Cheese Tomato Salad, 75
    Spinach Salad with Peanut Dressing, 78
Sate, spicy pork, 56
Sauces
  chili, 71-72, 80
  for fudge cake, 132
  for ham loaf, 171
  hot pepper, 71-72
  peanut butter, see Peanut butter sauce
  soy, 33-34, 38-39, 46, 56, 73, 82, 83, 85, 87
  tomato, see Tomato sauce
Scallops in fish fry, 59-60
Scottish Peanut Butter Scones with Lemon Curd, 100
Sesame seeds
  in candy, 154-55
  in cookies, 101
Shrimp
  in Chicken and Seafood Indonesia, 60
  in fish fry, 59-60
  Tahiti, 58
Shrimp Tahiti, 58
Siwee, 66
Smelts in fish fry, 59-60
Snacks, see Appetizers
Sole fillets, Okefenokee, 58-59
Soufflé, chilled, 141
Soups, 28-31
  Cream of Peanut, 28
  Creamy Peanut Tomato Soup, 30
  Cold Peanut Butter Vegetable Potage, 29
  Peanut Soup Creole, 29
  Quick Peanut Soup, 30
  Sudanese Shorba, 31
Sour cream
  in cream cheese tomato salad, 75
  in dessert, 140

Sour Cream *(cont.)*
  in dips, 22
  in Peanutty Festival
    Squash, 70
  in sauce, 84, 86
Sour Cream Chiffon Pie, 143
Southern Ragout, 44-45
Southern Sweet Potato-
  Peanut Butter
  Casserole, 65-66
Soy sauce, 33-34, 38-39, 46,
  56, 73, 82, 83, 85, 87
  peanut-, 73
Spaghetti, baked, 62
Spice Cupcakes, 125-26
Spiced Fruit Peanut Stuffing,
  54-55
Spicy Chicken Livers Southeast, 41
Spicy Chuck Roast, 45
Spicy Pork Sate, 56
Spinach Afrique, 69
Spinach Salad with Peanut
  Dressing, 78
Squash
  acorn, peanut filled, 69-70
  peanutty, 70
Stews
  Ghanian Stew, 44
  Southern Ragout, 44-45
  lamb, 41-42
Strawberries
  in fruit salad, 77-78
  in mayonnaise, 78-79
Strawberry-Peanut Mayonnaise, 78-79
Stuffed Sweet Potatoes with
  Peanut Butter, 67
Sudanese Shorba, 31
Superior Peanut Butter
  Cookies, 111
Sweet potatoes (yams)
  and bananas, African, 65
  in baked ham rolls, 52-53
  with beef stew, 44
  casserole, 65-66
  in Chicken Moamba, 37
  chicken pie with crust of,
    34-35
  peanut butter pork chop
    and, 55
  Siwee, 66
  stuffed, with peanut butter,
    67

Tabasco sauce, 19, 37-38,
  59-60, 69, 83, 85, 87
Tangy Fruitbread, 95
Tomato juice
  in chicken cutlets, 37-38
  in hush puppies and trout,
    57
  in peanut soup creole, 29
Tomato puree for spicy sauce,
  168
Tomato paste, 40
Tomato sauce, 41, 44-45, 47,
  52, 58, 63, 81-84
Tomato soup, creamy peanut,
  30
Tomatoes
  baked stuffed, 74
  in beef stew, 44
  in cheese dip, 24
  in chuck roast, 45
  in lamb stew, 41-42
  in peanut filled acorn
    squash, 69-70
  in Peanut Sauce Peruvian,
    85-86
  pork roast with, in sauce,
    53
  salad, with peanut butter
    and cream cheese, 75
  in Shrimp Tahiti, 58
  in Spinach Afrique, 69
  with veal, 48-50
  in vegetable platter, 71
Topping
  for Bride's Fingers, 108
  for cakes, 126-27, 134-35
  for chocolate sandwich
    cookies, 115-16
  for marshmallow squares,
    112

# INDEX

for peanut butter squares, 107
*See also* Frosting
Torte, ice-box, 147
Trout, fried, peanut butter hush puppies with, 57
Turkey leftovers in hash, 172

Vacherin, peanut-flavored, 126-27
Vanilla Peanut Butter Milk Shake, 164
Vanilla Peanut Divinity, 155
Veal
   chops, with spicy sauce, 49
   cutlets, with spicy sauce, 168

   Peruvian, 50
   roast, 48-49
Vegetable soup, cold, 29
Vegetables, 63-74
   Indonesian Vegetable Platter, 71
   in one-dish meal, 32-33
   Peanut Vegetable Loaf, 61-62
   *See also specific vegetables*

Wheat germ
   in beverage, 162-63
   in candy, 154-55
   in cookies, 101, 103
   in lentil burgers, 61

Yams, *see* Sweet potatoes